Jerusalem's Doctor of the Poor

Simon Majaro

Jerusalem's Doctor of the Poor

SML Publications
London

Designed and typeset by Robert Bigio.
Set in Joanna and Myriad Pro.

SML Publications
52D Maresfield Gardens
London NW3 5RX

ISBN 978-1-5262-0893-4

British Library Cataloguing in Publication Data

A catalogue record for this book is available from the British Library

For my grandchildren and great-grandchildren (present and future)

Preface

When my father reached the age of 90, and after 60 years of devoted medical care of his mixed constituency of Jews, Arabs and Christians the Municipality of Jerusalem awarded him a new title 'Dr. Leon Majaro, the Jerusalem Doctor of the Poor. He was thrilled by this. It represented for him the successful fulfilment of his aspirations and dreams, that guided him from the moment he left the Jaffa hospital, that saved his life.

I felt that this communal recognition opened an opportunity to re-tell the story of LM's life in the comfort of his happy and cultured home in Odessa plus the subsequent long and tortuous journey towards carving a successful career in Jerusalem. Throughout this long journey LM demonstrated enormous amount of grit and patience. The Municipality's award expressed its recognition of his achievement in a truly creative manner.

In his book From Odessa to Jerusalem LM provides a vivid description of life in Odessa in general and his own family. It makes fascinating reading. The book ends with LM visiting Jerusalem for the first time and deciding on the spot that he wished to settle there. It became his cherished dream. The next part of the journey was left untold in the book. I felt that I ought to fill this gap and briefly describe the remarkable journey he took to integrate himself into the country's culture, languages and demography.

The famous proverb says: 'It's an ill wind that blows nobody any good'. In March 2021 we were all affected by the dreadful Covid-19 pandemic. I was designated as a VAP (vulnerable adult person) and subject to a most rigorous isolation regime.

I decided to exploit my virtual 'house arrest' to write stories depicting my father's progress towards integration into the Jerusalem social and professional environments.

I also had an urge to write about events and situations from my own school days and anecdotes from home.

I am at an age in which my memory goes AWOL from time to time. Strangely, while my short-term memory lets me down occasionally my long-term memory is remarkably good. I may find it difficult to remember what I did yesterday but I can still remember the names of the children who were in my kindergarten class, or at least half of them.

A few of the stories are amusing, others are tragic but they all relate to the realities of the country under the British Mandate, which had its mixed moments of tranquillity and turmoil in quick succession.

Contents

Above: Odessa, about 1850. The Potemkin Steps are visible in the centre of the image.
Below: The Potemkin Steps today.

Growing up in Odessa

My father, Leon Majaro, was born in Odessa in 1892. At birth his name was Lev Mojarowsky. In common with most Russian children he was given a diminutive, in his case Liova. Lev means Lion and that is how he became Leon years later when he settled in Jerusalem.

Odessa at the time of his birth was a thriving part of the Tzar's empire. It was the only harbour in the whole empire designated as a 'warm water port' that enjoyed a year-round open navigation, unlike the main harbours in the Baltic north that suffered frequent interruptions of shipping during the winters when the sea froze. Odessa became the main port for distributing the empire's massive grain export.

Odessa over the centuries was a small garrison town and trading centre that changed hands many times. At one stage it belonged to the Tatars; later the Lithuanian Duchy stepped in to have access to the warm water harbour and finally it was absorbed by the Turks into the Ottoman Empire. At no stage did it flourish into a large prosperous town for a large civilian population.

Under the influence of Prince Potemkin, the Tsarina Catherine the Great decided to occupy the Turkish garrison and develop it into a significant city on the Black Sea, thus opening a gate for Russia into the warm water arena.

In 1792 during the Russo-Turkish War the Russian Army occupied the Turkish fort and it was immediately re-named Odessa.

The authorities faced the major problem that the area was devoid of a population able and willing to develop a major commercial and cultural metropolis. Under the guidance of Potemkin a range of incentives were offered to potential immigrants from other parts of the Empire. In particular some liberalisation of the very restrictive regime that plagued the Jewish community in the so-called 'Pale of Settlement' (a specific area where Jews were permitted to live) was a spur for Jews to move to Odessa. In Odessa the newly established education and professional worlds opened for them and they could practice in most trades and professions without restrictions.

Not surprisingly as Odessa developed its Jewish population grew as well and at its peak the Jewish community in Odessa comprised over a third of the total population.

Gradually Odessa became a most successful trading area coupled with a highly developed education system and cultural intellectual environments. Odessa became the envy of most large cities in Russia and beyond.

During the 19th century, Odessa was the fourth largest city of Imperial Russia, after Moscow, Saint Petersburg and Warsaw.

Odessa became a beautiful and prosperous city.
Above: Passage shopping arcade, where Simion Mojarowsky had a bookshop. *Below:* Odessa Opera House.

Left: Anna and Simion Mojarowsky.
Right: German (Herman) Blumenfeld, Anna's brother (by courtesy of Asya Gelfer).

The Mojarowsky ancestors were among the early Jewish settlers in Odessa and its surroundings. By the time Liova was born they were well established. His father Simion was a lawyer who became a director and part-owner of the famous local newspaper Odesky Novosty.

His mother, Anna, was a graduate in music of the local conservatoire and became a piano teacher. Her maiden name was Blumenfeld and her brother Herman (pronounced in Russia as German) Blumenfeld became a top lawyer in land law matters both in Odessa and the rest of the Empire. He earned the wonderful sobriquet: 'If Blumenfeld accepts your case – you have won…'

Liova's only sister Nadya (Nadejda) was a successful pianist and occasional composer. Liova himself was an outstanding scholar at the Gymnasium and played the violin to a very high standard. Throughout his school years he was not sure whether he wanted to become a doctor or a professional violinist.

Café Fankoni in Odessa, where the editorial committee of Odesky Novosty would meet. Simion Mojarowsky, part-owner of this paper, may be in this picture.

In his book *From Odessa to Jerusalem* Liova describes in vivid detail the kind of privileged life the people known as the Odessa Intelligentsia enjoyed prior to the First world War.

Despite the liberalisation of most of the restrictions on Jewish occupations and activities it was still necessary for young Jewish students wishing to join a university to emerge from the Gymnasium with a gold medal. Jewish students therefore worked extremely hard to achieve such an accolade. Liova achieved that level of excellence and decided to study medicine at the Odessa University instead of pursuing a musical career. Before graduation he also spent a few terms in a German medical school.

Nadya and Liova.

Liova graduated in 1916 as a young doctor while World War I was raging throughout Europe. Straight from university, and prior to gaining sufficient practical experience, he was recruited into the Russian Army.

On joining the Army he was given two choices: the German front or the Turkish front. Most young doctors chose the former inasmuch as it was known that the journey from the front to Odessa by train was pretty short and it was possible to grab the occasional visit to Odessa. The Turkish front was avoided because it was known that a serious epidemic of typhus was causing havoc among the troops and it was also located a long distance away in Eastern Anatolia with appalling Transport facilities. Going home for an occasional weekend break was out of the question.

Liova chose the Turkish front. His parents were devastated, fearing that they might never see him again.

Liova's decision to select the Turkish arena was partially due to a deep-rooted fascination with the Orient. It also illustrated an intrepid personality. Fearlessness became a major trait throughout his future life. To that extent becoming a doctor for Cossack soldiers, known for their fearlessness, attracted him.

Liova: doctor of a Cossack brigade

The doctor of a Cossack brigade

The Russian Army and the Cossack Brigade were stationed around a city called Erzerum in Eastern Anatolia. Erzerum is situated at 1900 metres (6233 feet) above sea level and suffers harsh winters. Today Erzerum has become a ski resort.

By the time Liova reached the Brigade's headquarters military operations had ceased. Following the brilliant naval Battle of Trebizond on the Black Sea the Ottoman troops abandoned the whole province to the Russian Army on 15 April 1916. This coincided with Liova's arrival.

Being a Cossack Brigade's doctor in a no-fighting zone meant that his medical duties centred around infrequent and simple maladies of strong and healthy soldiers.

However the typhus cases that were endemic in the camp gradually grew into an epidemic. Liova's duties were transformed from GP work to a day-and-night battle against the dreaded lice that were responsible for the transmission of the disease.

A lot of his work necessitated rigorous educational preventative campaigns to locate and eradicate the lice on the body of every soldier. Once a soldier was infected the hope of survival in those conditions was grim. Sick soldiers were dying every day. For a young doctor the whole experience was traumatic.

In the middle of all this, as Liova used to tell, was the sad story of his involvement in the execution of a soldier sentenced to death by a court martial. The exact circumstances are not known but it appears that it had political treasonous undertones. At the time some revolutionary sentiments had started simmering in the Russian society. The condemned soldier was executed by a firing squad. Liova's only role as a doctor was to certify that the victim was dead. This was purely an independent professional certification of death.

Nonetheless on leaving the scene a soldier muttered: 'Doctor, you will live to regret it'. Liova realised that this was a political statement and threat. He was in no way involved with the Court Martial and the verdict. As a doctor soldier he was performing a duty.

The menacing words left their mark on Liova. He realised that should the communists or allies take over the country he would be branded by them as an undesirable person.

The end of the war

In October of 1917, Lenin took full control of the government in what is called the Bolshevik Revolution. Russia was now the first communist country in the world. After the revolution, Russia exited World War I by signing a peace treaty with Germany called the Treaty of Brest-Litovsk.

On March 3, 1918, in the city of Brest-Litovsk, located in modern-day Belarus near the Polish border, Russia signed a treaty with the Central Powers ending its participation in World War I.

The revolution caused a catastrophic deterioration in the economy and infrastructural services. The Russian Army disintegrated, and soldiers were literally told to go home. Organised demobilisation hardly existed. the country was verging on a civil war between the Bolsheviks (the Reds) and the supporters of the old regime (the Whites). In the middle of these anarchical circumstances Liova started his long trek home.

It took him weeks to reach Odessa. He travelled by a variety of means ranging from walking, lifts on peasants' horse-drawn

Simion Mojarowsky

carts and short train journeys when available. Ultimately, totally exhausted, he reached Odessa.

Liova's parents were delighted and greatly relieved to see him again. After a well-needed shower and short rest his father took Liova aside and addressed his beloved only son:

'My dear Liova, as soon as you feel fully recovered from your nightmarish track home, I suggest you pack your bags and leave this country. Go anywhere you like. This country will become hell on earth for many years. You are young enough to start a new life somewhere away from this forthcoming maelstrom. Just get out'.

This was sad and prescient advice to one's only son.

Leaving Odessa

The obvious first step on leaving Russia from Odessa, on the Black Sea, was the short sea trip to Constantinople in Turkey (later re-named Istanbul). Liova took the short trip in a Russian ship and landed in Constantinople in April 1918.

Spending a few weeks in a small Constantinople hotel he examined carefully the destination options open to him.

He soon discovered that a fairly large number of Jewish refugees from Palestine were stuck in Turkey. These were Jewish citizens from Tel Aviv and Jaffa who were deported en masse to Turkey by the Ottoman Government in Palestine. The Ottoman Authorities were convinced that the whole Jewish population were potential spies for the British Army advancing from Egypt to Palestine. Deporting them to Turkey, they felt, would keep them out of mischief.

Once the War was over, with the British having occupied Palestine and established a British Mandated state there, all the Jewish deportees in Turkey were eager to return home.

The Argenfels, the ship that took Liova to Palestine.

The Jewish Agency and a number of Jewish charities chartered a ship by the name of SS Argenfels to transport the exiles to Jaffa.

In the light of this scenario, and remembering that he was a Jew, Liova decided that seeking to make his way to the Holy Land was a good choice.

Through some cunning moves Liova managed to masquerade as a Jewish deportee and succeeded in joining one of the journeys to Jaffa via Beirut on the Argenfels.

Among the passengers there were also a few Arabs, who had served in the Ottoman Army returning home to Syria and The Lebanon – hence the stop in Beirut.

Liova was the only doctor on board the ship during his trip. The ship had to zig-zag slowly to avoid the many mine fields installed by the Ottomans during the war. The trip lasted a lot longer than planned.

Sadly, cases of typhus flared up during the journey, especially among the Arab soldiers who had recently returned from the various battlefields. Being the only doctor on the ship Liova was asked to provide medical help and guidance. A few of the patients died and the captain insisted on burying them at sea, the accepted tradition in the maritime world at the time.

After a brief stop at Beirut harbour for the Arab soldiers to disembark the ship continued its tortuous journey to Jaffa.

Arriving in Jaffa most of the Jewish returnees were greeted by jubilant friends and relatives. Liova was a lonely stranger disembarking without a single person to welcome him.

He felt extremely unwell. He had a terrible feeling that this time his exposure to soldiers with Typhus infected him due to lack of sanitary facilities on board the ship.

Sweating and trembling, and with the generous help of one of the passengers, he managed to drag himself into a Jewish hotel. Luckily the owner realised immediately that the guest was very sick and arranged to have him moved to a Jewish hospital by the name of Shaar Tzion. This was a stroke of luck.

Liova was desperately ill for six weeks. At one stage the doctors feared that he would not survive. Thanks to most dedicated and caring doctors and nurses he managed a slow return to health. In any other hospital he would have probably died.

Shimon Rokach.

The lucky part of the whole episode was the fact that during his illness he was visited a couple of times by a gentleman by the name of Shimon Rokach, who happened to be one of the founders of the Shaar Tzion hospital and was one of its governors. Liova was unaware that Rokach was the head of the Jewish community in Jaffa and Neve Tzedek.

Mr. Rokach noticed that Liova had a violin under the bed. 'Doctor, when you recover please come and visit us at Neve Tzedek. My daughter Hannah plays the piano.' He gave Liova his card which proved to be a most fortuitous entrée into Tel Aviv's top society.

Making a career as a young doctor in Palestine

Having survived a nasty episode of typhus in the Shaar Tzion Hospital, Liova, at the age of 27, emerged into the real world of Tel Aviv. He was still weak, lonely and short of funds.

The Russian Roubles and the Turkish Pounds he brought with him were plummeting at an alarming rate. The only useful cash he had in his possession was a small stack of pounds sterling. It was sufficient to sustain him for a few weeks only. The need to settle into a profitable activity had become very urgent.

Liova was seriously handicapped by not being able to communicate in the three official languages of the country: English, Hebrew and Arabic. He spoke fluent Russian, French and some German but these languages were not helpful in seeking to communicate with the British authorities or any Arabic or Hebrew speakers.

His first attempt to establish himself as a practising doctor in Tel Aviv was not successful.

Tel Aviv had at the time eight doctors. For a young doctor wishing to establish himself in such a competitive environment it was essential to be able to offer a unique speciality.

A street scene in Tel Aviv in the 1920s.

Dr. Sherman, the doyen of the local medical fraternity, who tried to help Liova, suggested that Tel Aviv needed a neurologist inasmuch as many Tel Avivians, he claimed, were 'mentally deranged'. Liova started swatting his medical books for extra knowledge on neurological conditions. From a small room in a well-known Hotel Hoz he set up his surgery. Despite all his efforts to market his services, including a poster on a popular noticeboard, few individuals turned up with mental problems to the new 'expert' in town.

Learning Hebrew in Ben Shemen

Liova realised that his first challenge was to learn the basics of the three official languages with some urgency. He knew that unless he learned the rudiments of the three languages his career would suffer badly.

In a fascinating book *Lod* (the Hebrew name for the biblical town of Lydda), written by Liova in Hebrew but not yet translated into English, he describes most vividly the various

Ben Shemen Moshav in the 1920s, remote and isolated.

remarkable initiatives he undertook in order to force him to learn the three languages in quick succession.

One of the doctors in Tel Aviv informed Liova that there was a temporary job for a resident doctor in a Moshav (agricultural village) and youth village by the name of Ben Shemen. Ben Shemen was located 3km east of Lydda in the vicinity of the main road to Jerusalem.

In these pleasant surroundings Liova assumed the role of a GP including the occasional nursing for minor injuries. He had to learn Hebrew quickly to be able to communicate with the local members and pupils. He was popular among the residents and made good progress in learning the basics of Hebrew.

Ben Shemen Moshav in 1911, six years after it was founded.

Learning Arabic in Lydda

Now he needed to learn Arabic. While chatting with the senior members of the village he discovered that the neighbouring town of Lydda was desperate to have a doctor in their midst.

The town of Lydda had only a few hundred families at the beginning of the century but expanded quickly and in 1919 became important railway junction. It had about 17,000 inhabitants, one-fifth Christians and the rest Arab Muslims.

Lydda had an important attraction for Liova. As a railway junction it offered frequent railway connections to Jaffa. It meant that had he decided to settle in Lydda he could still maintain frequent visits to friends in Tel Aviv and Jaffa. In particular he could keep contact with the Rokach family and their daughter Hannah, with whom he had managed to establish a warm relationship.

One fine day he plucked courage and walked the 3 kms from Ben Shemen to Lydda to explore the opportunities to work among the Arab population there.

St George's Church, Lydda.

It was a further example of his intrepid personality. For a young Russian doctor, unfamiliar with the habits and customs of the local Arab population, and not speaking the language, it was foolhardy to expect to find work in such circumstances.

Nonetheless, with his enormous charm and determination he succeeded.

On arriving at Lydda's central square, he entered the most prominent café and ordered a coffee. The shop was empty at the time and the owner was intrigued by this strange foreigner. Out of curiosity he tried to start a conversation. He soon realised

The barber, the young assistant and the new doctor in Lydda.

that there was a serious language barrier but also discovered that the guest spoke German. 'I shall call my brother, he speaks German because he went to the German Missionary Schneler School in Jerusalem.' Eureka! now a meaningful dialogue could start as soon as the German-speaking brother arrived.

From this first contact things progressed at some speed.

The town was desperate for a local resident doctor. The only medical service available was a twice-weekly visit by a doctor from Jaffa. These visits were happening at irregular intervals.

It was agreed that Liova would move to Lydda and settle into suitable digs in the smarter part of the town. A barber situated next to the café was willing to set aside part of his shop as the doctor's surgery for a few hours every day at a small fee.

Abdullah, a young barber assistant, agreed to act as the doctor's helper for a small fee. He proved to be a brilliant and loyal aide. He acted as a receptionist, prepared meals for the doctor, mixed drugs to the doctor's orders and collected the doctor's fees for the consultations and drugs. He was a true delight.

The idea was for Liova to assume the role of a 'dispensing doctor' thus acting both as a doctor and as pharmacist. The town did not have a local pharmacy. Liova travelled from time to time to Jaffa and acquired a stock of popular medicines and pharmaceutical components for mixing his own prescriptions.

In his book Lod (Lydda) Liova describes many interesting and charming episodes that he experienced in his practice. Abdullah acted as the translator until Liova picked up enough Arabic to communicate direct with the patients. He learned a lot about the customs and attitudes of his patients who were in the main simple, honest and uneducated agricultural workers. He discovered that most of his patients were reluctant to tell the doctor what was wrong with them. They believed that a clever doctor should find out everything through examination.

He tells the poignant story of a fellow who refrained from telling the doctor that he had been bitten by a rabid dog. A simple admission of the fact would have explained all the symptoms and would have saved the patient's life.

Dr Leon Majaro in Lydda.

Liova's period in Lydda was a success. He was loved and respected by the locals. He earned fairly good income and he picked up enough Arabic to be able to converse with Arab patients with confidence. He never encountered a single hostile hint or innuendo about his Jewish background during his time in Lydda.

Altogether he enjoyed the experience enormously. The relative proximity of Lydda to Jaffa enabled him to maintain contact with the Rokach family at Neve Tzedek. By the end of a year Liova's spoken Arabic became fairly fluent and his rapport with Arab patients was excellent.

Joining the Palestine Government's Health Department

One day Liova was summoned to the government's health department to discuss a potential position in medical borders control. He had approached the medical department earlier about this but they had no vacancies at the time.

The job on offer was to join a team of doctors and paramedics to monitor and control the status of hygiene and health of passengers arriving in Palestine by sea, air and rail. The aim was to identify early signs of potential carriers of dangerous illnesses. Allegedly the great risk was attributed to the many Arabs returning by rail via Egypt from their Hijrah to Mecca and Medina. These pilgrims spent many weeks in most unhygienic conditions and there was a real danger that a few of them might harbour the seeds of a serious epidemic.

Liova accepted the position and signed a contract for one year with the Palestine government's health department. He was now a salaried civil servant.

Before leaving his friends in Lydda he found a young German doctor who was willing and eager to take over his practice immediately.

His first few jobs as Medical Borders Controller was to board ships arriving at Jaffa and check with the ships' captains and crew the detailed medical history during their recent journey. Were there any illnesses on board? Did any passengers die and have to be buried at sea? Were there any passengers who required a quarantine order?

This initial stage was very interesting and enjoyable. It also meant that he could keep in touch with his friends in Tel Aviv and especially his lady-friend Hannah Rokach.

The next step was much more complicated and uncomfortable. He was transferred to manage the medical control at the border between Egypt and Palestine, centred in a railway town called Kantara (El Cantara in Arabic).

Kantara was a major supply depot of the British Army on the Suez Canal. The British improved the whole system because it was an essential part of the army's logistics in the that area.

Kantara itself comprised of two halves: Kantara West (in Egypt) and Kantara East (in Palestine). Trains from Cairo and Alexandria terminated at the Western station on the Suez Canal. Passengers crossed a bridge over the Suez Canal or were ferried to the Kantara East to catch a Palestinian train that would travel along the Mediterranean coast via Rafah to Gaza and on to Jaffa. Later it could proceed to Haifa.

Liova and a few colleagues were responsible for the monitoring the health history of the passengers in Kantara while the customs and immigration personnel were doing their work. It was not unusual for Jewish people returning from a visit to

Hannah Rokach with a photograph of her father, Shimon.

Europe to travel via Alexandria and take the train to Kantara, cross the Suez Canal and proceed to Jaffa. Liova recounted in his book of an occasion when Shimon Rokach and a few members of the family returned home, from a holiday in Europe, via this route and had to pass through his medical controlling procedures.

Accommodation provided was rather spartan, being in a large tent attached to the military depot in Kantara East.

In a smaller adjoining tent he was offered the services of a batman-helper to provide him with food and deal with other domestic chores. The job itself was interesting and he was learning basic English from his British colleagues on duty.

The one fly in the ointment was the fact that it was far away from Tel Aviv and his dear girlfriend Hannah. They agreed to correspond frequently and retain close contact. Liova now having a free travel pass on the trains promised to come to Tel Aviv from time to time although the journey was long.

For some unknown reason the frequency of letters from Hannah ceased and Liova got very worried. He decided to travel to Tel Aviv after completing his inspection shift on the Kantara–Rafah train section. Without seeking permission from his superior he decided to stay on the train going north to Jaffa and Tel Aviv.

During a brief stop at Rafah a massive explosion shook the train and the whole surroundings. The source of the explosion was unknown. Only on reaching Jaffa he heard that an enormous explosion took place in the British army depot and arsenal with many casualties.

The Kantarah–Rafah train at Lydda Station during the British Mandate.

It later transpired that Liova's batman was decapitated and his tent and all his personal possessions wiped out. Luckily Liova had his violin with him on the train.

Clearly Liova's AWOL was a very lucky escape but he was very worried that his superiors may take a very dim view of his absence without leave and punish him accordingly.

Liova's first port of call on reaching Tel Aviv was the home of the Rokach family in Neve Tzedek. The whole family welcomed him with open arms and considered that his miraculous escape from the depot's inferno was a providential blessing.

The family celebrated this miracle with great joy. The situation morphed into an unexpected happy occasion: the engagement and forthcoming marriage of Liova and Hannah was announced.

The next day, with trepidation, Liova called on the local health department office, his employers. He expected to be fired. The local head, Major Harkness, literally jumped with joy to see him: 'We all thought that you were killed during the dreadful explosion. Wonderful to see you alive.' His fear of punishment for being absent without leave vanished.

At the same time the health department decided to transfer Liova from his Kantara duties to a large government hospital for infectious diseases in Haifa. A most welcome change.

Having survived a cataclysmic accident and having announced the engagement to his beloved Hannah, he was ready to start a new chapter in the process of taking roots in the Holy Land.

His hope of ultimately settling down in Jerusalem was still very much alive and by now he spoke Hebrew, Arabic and English in addition to his other languages.

The wedding in Haifa

On 16 November 1920 Liova went to the Haifa railway station to welcome the whole Rokach family who came to the wedding of Hannah and Liova in the Herzlia Hotel in Haifa.

The only member of the family missing was Israel, Hannah's younger brother, who was pursuing a post-graduate electric engineering programme in London.

Due to the fact that Liova's job was now centred in the Government's Haifa's Hospital for Infectious Diseases the young couple settled in Haifa. However they both longed for an opportunity to move to Jerusalem.

This was realised when received an offer to become the doctor in charge of Bikur Holim a Jewish hospital in the Old City of Jerusalem. This invitation was engineered by a distant cousin of the Rokach family who was the head of the famous Yeshiva Etz Haim and also a member of the hospital's governing board. The attraction of the job was that it included a spacious apartment on the ground floor of the building and a separate surgery where Liova could run a private GP practice.

Hannah and Liova on their wedding day.

The hospital was situated in the Armenian Quarter of the Old City, next to both the Jewish and Muslim Quarters. It was evident that establishing a private surgery in such an area would guarantee a busy multifarious practice for a general practitioner. The nearest other doctors were in the Jewish Quarter.

A mural depicting the founders of Neve Tzedek, with Hannah's father Shimon in the centre.

Liova was very excited at the prospect of having such a diverse clientele. A further bonus was that the Hospital had its own pharmacy with a full-time pharmacist.

After signing a contract with Bikur Holim he gave notice to the Department of Health, his current employers, and started planning a move to Jerusalem, which became his home for the next 70 years.

ד״ר ל. מג׳רו
Dr L. MAJARO
الدكتور موجاره

Settling in Jerusalem

Liova and Hannah moved to Jerusalem in great anticipation of an exciting life in the heart of the ancient old city.

For Liova it was a natural evolution towards a steady and promising career development. By now he had become fairly fluent in the country's three languages which boded well for running a GP practice with a multi-ethnic and multi-lingual clientele. This appealed to Liova.

For Hannah moving to the Old City of Jerusalem was a great new adventure. As a very sociable person she was looking forward to meeting interesting people, especially among the cultural and music-loving Armenian community next door to the hospital. In addition a significant number of senior British Government civil servants decided to settle in the neighbourhood and Hannah became a popular hostess among them.

He soon discovered that his Arab patients finding the name Mojarowsky a bit of a mouthful and started calling him 'The Russian Doctor'. Liova did not like this title and decided to drop the WSKY thus re-branding himself as Mojaro, an easier name to remember.

Alas, when he went to the appropriate Government office, which dealt with name changes, the clerk made a mistake and wrote the new name as Majaro. My absent-minded father missed the mistake. It was only when he reached home that my very alert mother noticed it. A long debate followed as to whether another trip to the Registrar of Names was needed. The result was that they ultimately agreed that Majaro sounds better than Mojaro. Little they knew at the time that Majaro is a well-known Nigerian name. One of the main streets in Lagos is named Majaro Street.

At this point I shall stop talking about Liova Mojarowsky and continue with the new appellation Dr. Leon Majaro. Under this name he became known as a popular GP throughout his career in Jerusalem, both in the Old City and later in the new parts of Jerusalem. I shall use the simple moniker LM from now onwards in this narrative.

LM was a quiet and shy man. Throughout his life he tended to shun the limelight and preferred to live and work as a general practitioner in modest surroundings. The major part of his career he spent as a doctor in the Old City of Jerusalem. He became known as Jerusalem's doctor of the poor. His patients were a mixture of Jews, Arabs and Christians. The majority of them were poor residents of old Jerusalem. The more affluent ones moved to the new suburbs. All his patients loved and respected him. In turn he was immensely caring and loyal to his patients.

Bikur Holim Hospital in Old Jerusalem

Dr. Leon Majaro was a hard-working conscientious medical practitioner. In addition to being the doctor in charge of a hospital in the Old City of Jerusalem he ran a GP practice in the ground floor of the hospital and also in a dedicated separate part of our apartment in west Jerusalem.

The hospital, Bikur Holim ('visiting the sick') was established in the Old City of Jerusalem in 1826 in a large ramshackle Arab building, which was refurbished to a fairly high standard. Its aim was to provide local hospital facilities for the Jewish community in the Old City and also a day surgery for all the neighbouring communities – Jews, Arabs and Christians. Dr. Majaro was in charge of the medical sides of both from 1920 until the hospital had to be moved to the modern Jerusalem, under British Army escort during the war of independence in 1948.

The charity responsible for the management of Bikur Holim enjoyed generous support from Sir Moses Montefiore, especially in the provision of medicines.

Bikur Holim Hospital in Jerusalem.

Jerusalem was developing rapidly outside the city walls and many Jews migrated from the Old City Jewish quarters to the modern west side of the City.

The directors of Bikur Holim decided to establish a major hospital in the modern part of Jerusalem. This happened in stages in the early part of the 20th Century. At this point the hospital in the Old City was downgraded into a medical shelter for chronic and terminal cases and geriatric patients.

Among the permanent patients in the re-formed old Bikur Holim was a small contingent of victims of the dreaded epidemic, known as encephalitis lethargica or 'sleeping sickness' that had taken place throughout the world, simultaneously with the Spanish flu pandemic. Millions were infected by the encephalitis plague, especially during 1917. The disease affects the nervous system and plunges the victims into many months or even years of zombie-like frozen slumber and paralysis.

The famous work of Dr. Oliver Sacks, and his wonderful book Awakenings, summarised his heroic endeavours to return victims of this scourge from their unfortunate slumber to the real world (first published in 1973, revised edition 1990).

A number of religious Jewish families in Europe and US opted to transfer their beloved victims to the Bikur Holim in the Old City of Jerusalem for long-term care. They appreciated the fact that it was a Jewish hospital with religious rituals followed conscientiously. They were impressed by the medical attention and care provided by the hospital's team under the direction of Dr. Leon Majaro and his assistants. A few of these long-term patients were awake and able to communicate with some difficulty although totally immobilised.

One individual by the name of Mr. Levinson was paralysed below the waist and spent his time in bed or in a wheelchair but miraculously was able to draw and paint. As a young boy I used to visit the hospital with my father and had my portrait painted by Levinson. He also drew a portrait of my sister. Both were excellent and are on display at our family's Museum in my grandfather's house in Neve Tzedek, Tel-Aviv.

Dr. Majaro looked after the encephalitis group with care and attention, almost as if they were members of his own family. In turn, those who could, reciprocated by expressing their affection for him. I was always impressed, when I escorted my father on our periodic visits, the way he was met by an adoring smile round the wards.

LM was a modest person and consistently avoided the limelight. He enjoyed his work and his loyal clientele. At no stage did he aspire to move to the big hospitals away from the Old City. With his family connections he could have 'engineered' a move to one of the major medical centres. He was determined to continue to serve his large and devoted multi-faceted congregation. He appreciated the professional freedom that the situation allowed him.

On reaching the age of 90, the Jerusalem Town Hall bestowed upon him an honorary award coupled with the title 'Dr. Leon Majaro – the Doctor of the Poor'.

Being a 'Jerusalem Doctor of the Poor' is not a formula for amassing wealth. The combined income from the hospital and the GP practices provided my father and family with enough income to lead a frugal existence. As a modest 'top up' my mother had some extra income from the family's orange groves.

My father never took any interest in financial matters. He never explored possibilities of investing in the stock market or other long-term financial vehicles.

Nonetheless he was proud of two exceptions to this reluctance to become 'better off'.

He was highly gratified that at an early stage of his marriage he acquired, at a relatively high expense, two burial plots in the Mount of Olives for himself and his wife Hannah. Being buried in the cherished and priceless cemetery of the glorious Mount of Olives was always the dream of every Jerusalemite. For my father it was the nearest he ever indulged himself in a significant and astute financial transaction. He used to aver that in the future only multi-millionaires could hope to pay the entry price for this hallowed eternal Jewish resting necropolis.

The other asset he was proud of was his cherished violin.

As a promising young violinist his father bought for him a violin. The label inside said 'Stradivarius fecit'...

I have no idea what the family paid for it but with such a clear-cut provenance an innocent owner was entitled to bask in the dream that one possessed a hidden fortune.

My father and his violin were inseparable.

During the WWI the violin escorted my father to the Turkish front where he served as a doctor of a Cossack brigade. Later the violin travelled with him to the Holy Land where he savoured his romance with my mother, Hannah Rokach, by playing violin and piano duets.

Thus Leon had two assets that gave him the feeling of some affluence: a prestigious family burial plot in Mount of Olives and a Stradivarius violin. Each of these assets had its subsequent history and deserves separate stories.

Mount of Olives cemetery.

Mount of Olives

My mother Hannah Rokach Majaro passed away in 1982 at the age of 88. A few months later my father Dr. Leon Majaro passed away at the age of 91.

They were buried next to each other in the precious family-owned last resting place. Elegant marble gravestones were commissioned and installed. My father's dream was fulfilled.

In 2006, on one of my visits to Jerusalem, I invited my grandson Jonathan to join me on the trip. It was his first visit to Israel and to Jerusalem. I decided to include a visit to the graves of my parents in the Mount of Olives. The vast cemetery of the Mount of Olives, where scores of generations of Jewish people are buried, is a fascinating location with an incredible panorama of the whole of Jerusalem.

On this occasion I encountered a problem: our visit coincided with the tail end of the so-called El-Aqsa Intifada.

Not far from my parents' graves an Arab village was situated. I was very reluctant to continue our visit without a suitable bodyguard. I phoned the management of the site and explained my worry. 'Don't worry', they assured me. 'We shall arrange for armed escorts to be present when you come. Just let us know your planned time of arrival'.

We arrived by taxi at the appointed time and to our amazement a platoon of armed IDF soldiers was waiting for us. I was totally reassured and impressed.

A short walk among the myriad of tombs of countless ages brought us to the spot where my parents' graves glistened in their relative newness. WOW! I was abruptly taken aback when my eye caught the gravestone of my parents' cheek-by-jowl neighbour: ROBERT MAXWELL died 1991.

I was speechless and was hurled into a sombre reflective mood. How would my dear parents react to being buried next to such a notorious giant crook? When you invest in a burial plot you never know who your neighbour is likely to be. I am glad that my parents did not know about their infamous neighbour.

Obviously 'money talks'. On this occasion the Maxwell family managed to acquire a plot next to my parents. During his funeral the Prime Minister Shamir and President Herzog attended with six leaders and previous leaders of the Mossad. Why?

'Stradivarius fecit'

On one of my trips to Jerusalem, following my father's death, I decided to bring the instrument to London in order to investigate its true background, provenance and value.

I felt that London had a better choice of experts and auction houses dealing with string instruments than Israel.

The violin was in a very neglected condition. It has not been played for a few years. It needed a new bridge; re-gluing of the finger-board; new strings; re-aligning the sound-post and general maintenance. I felt that before calling on the many expert dealers and auction houses I ought to restore the instrument to its earlier state. I spent a few weekends undertaking this assignment with a lot of love and patience. At the end it looked good and the sound was excellent. Stradivarius would have been proud of me.

Visiting and talking to dealers and auction houses was quite an experience. Talking to four violin dealers is like talking to four estate agents when you are trying to sell your house.

The one unanimous verdict was that the violin was not made by Stradivarius. They all maintained that the label 'Stradivarius fecit' only meant that it was a copied Stradivarius model.

I persevered until I came across a very knowledgeable dealer who pin-pointed the maker as a member of a well-known family of luthiers in Mittenwald, Germany, by the name of Horensteiner. They specialised for many years in making copies of Stradivarius models.

The Hornsteiner range was very popular with young musicians and advanced students. The quality was regarded as 'excellent value for money'. The price was fairly modest and certainly not millions.

My father's second rich possession did not live up to its dreams. The violin is in my possession and I cherish it as a dear family relic, albeit, sadly, not what it purports to be.

The family grows

On 6 May 1926 the Majaros celebrated the happy arrival of their first baby daughter named Leah.

The Bikur Holim hospital in the Old City gradually changed its character to a caring unit for disabled geriatrics and incurable diseases, in addition to the contingent of the victims of the encephalitis plague.

Bikur Holim set up a new hospital in the modern western part of the city outside the walls of the Old City. LM refused to budge to the new hospital and decided to soldier on with his mission to care for the helpless inmates of the old hospital plus his very busy GP practice, which continued to thrive.

The family was well-settled in these strange surroundings and managed to engineer for themselves a certain amount of social and cultural life. LM and Hannah often played duets – violin and piano sonatas, with baby Leah giggling in the background. Altogether these were happy days.

On 25 June 1929 the second baby, Shimon, was born. The arrival of the first boy in the larger Rokach family was a very welcome joyful event. Coincidentally he was named Shimon after both his grandparents – Shimon Rokach and Simion Mojarowsky.

The joy of Shimon's arrival was cut short by the very tragic events in the outside world. The happy days in the Old City came to an end for the Majaro family.

Shimon and Leah Majaro.

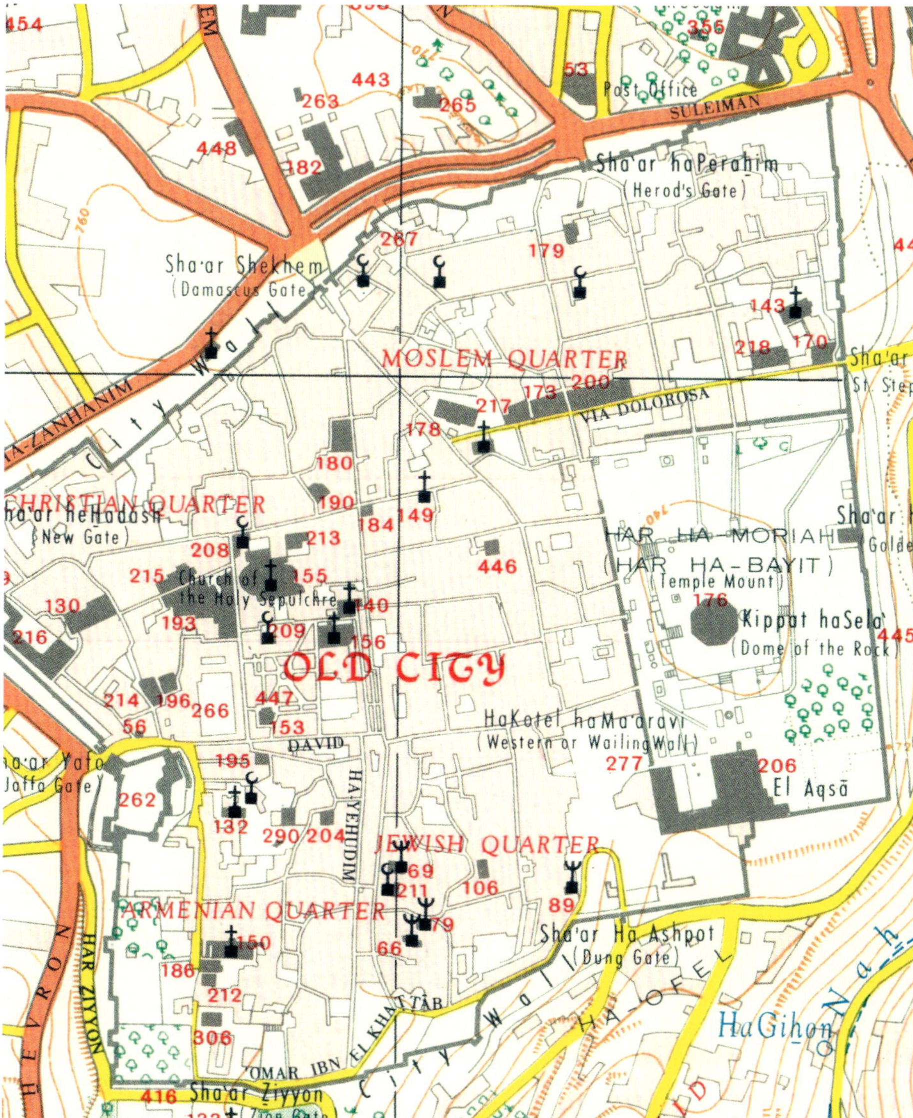

Map of Jerusalem in 1968, published by Survey of Israel.
Bikur Holim Hospital was in the Armenian Quarter, to the lower left of the map, and is marked with the number 290.
(From the collection of Eran Laor at the National Library of Israel.)

The Rokach family home, now a museum and home to the eminent artist Leah Majaro-Mintz, who restored the house.

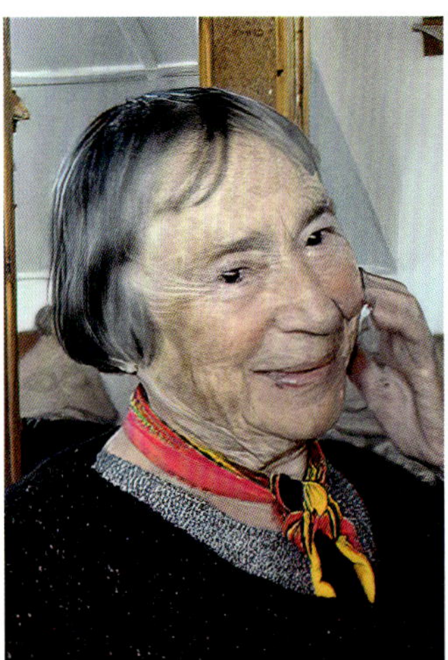

Leah Majaro-Mintz and some of her work in the back garden of Beit Rokach.

The 1929 Palestine riots and the Hebron massacre

The peace of the country came to an end with a savage series of demonstrations, riots and massacres perpetrated by Arabs against Jews in many parts of the country.

The riots consisted of attacks on Jews, mostly where their communities were isolated and defenceless. During the period 23–29 August 1929 ferocious attacks on Jewish areas accompanied by destruction of property and wholesale murder of residents including women and children.

On 24 August 1929 in Hebron, Arab mobs attacked the Jewish quarter killing men, women and children, raping women and looting Jewish property. They killed between 65 and 68 Jews in Hebron and wounded 58, with some of the victims being tortured, or mutilated.

Sir John Chancellor, the British High Commissioner visited Hebron and later commented, 'The horror of it is beyond words'. Many of the dead were students in the local Yeshiva.

A similar atrocity took place in the old Jewish Quarter of Safed. The Jewish Quarter was destroyed and many of its

Jewish inhabitants murdered or injured. Altogether 133 Jews were killed and around 200 injured by the Arab mobs. The Arabs sustained some casualties as a result of indiscriminate fire from British troops and police trying to stem the onslaught on the Jewish homes.

The bloody massacres and savage riots traumatised the Jewish community and left an abiding sense of beleaguerment and defencelessness.

The faith in the ability of the Mandatory Police and Army to defend isolated Jewish communities crumbled. This in turn spurred a national wish to establish, legally or illegally, a well-equipped Jewish defence organisation to deal with such future tragedies.

The Hebron massacre remained in the Jewish psyche a symbol of the kind of barbarity that part of the Arab community was capable of carrying out when stirred by the more ruthless leaders.

The desire to avenge this calamity was vocally expressed by members of the more extreme Jewish political leaders and remained so for many years. The whole series of events had a calamitous long-term impact on any attempts to build social and cultural bridges with the Arab neighbours.

Migration from the Old City

The situation provoked an exodus of Jewish families from the Old City to the newer and safer parts of west Jerusalem.

My parents decided to move from their spacious apartment in the hospital in the Old City following the dreadful massacre in Hebron in 1929. The location of the hospital in the midst of a hostile environment felt very unsafe.

The modern quarters in the newer parts of the west of the city felt distinctly safer inasmuch very few Arabs lived in those areas. Besides, in the newer districts the Jewish community established well-trained defence units.

While the Majaros decided to move their home away from the Old City, the hospital with all its patients remained behind. LM remained in charge and needed to attend for his normal duties plus his GP practice every day. This meant that he needed to walk or travel every day from the safe part of Jerusalem to the less safe one. For many years it caused us all great anxiety. On many occasions I remember the fear I harboured, when my father went to work in the Old City, that I may not see him again. A painful experience for a young boy.

In search of a suitable accommodation my parents looked for an area in which the demography was suitable for my father's medical practice. We moved from apartment to apartment until we settled in a flat with a garden in a street called Sfat Emet, meaning 'language of truth'. The name was given to the street because across the road from our flat it housed a very famous Yeshiva by that name. The Yeshiva was founded by the illustrious Hassidic 'Gerrer Rebbe' (Grand Rabbi Abraham Mordechai Alter , originally from the Ukraine).

Growing up in Jerusalem

Leah and I had a happy childhood. Jerusalem, on the whole, was a tranquil, cultured and interesting environment to live in.

Leah and I followed the traditional route from kindergartens, primary schools to the famous Hebrew Gymnasia of Jerusalem, allegedly the best senior school in town.

Alas the peace of the city was occasionally interrupted by murderous attacks in various parts of the city by Arab armed gangs, incited by a very hostile leadership. These attacks became frequent and dangerous during the period 1936–1939. That period was known as the 'Arab revolt' or simply the 'Troubles'.

The 'Troubles' came to an end at the beginning of WWII. Jerusalem was calm during the war and unlike Tel Aviv and Haifa, escaped attacks from the Italian or German planes.

After the war the Palestine problem became very complex and the British Mandatory Government found itself trapped into military hostility from both the Arab and the Jewish sides. Two brutal Jewish terror groups, Irgun and the Stern Gang, emerged and harassed the British administration and armed forces most ruthlessly with heavy casualties. Clearly these events impacted on the tranquillity of Jerusalem.

The whole situation unravelled into a decision by the British Government to hand over the whole problem to the United Nations and withdraw all its forces and administration from Palestine by April 1948.

The atmosphere in Jerusalem became stressful and unsafe. Great care was taken to avoid certain parts of the city which were deemed to be less safe.

A few of the next stories illustrate the climate which pervaded the life of our family.

The stories represent events, anecdotes and people that left a mark on me throughout my childhood and school. A few of these stories are amusing; others are tragic. All the stories stand alone as separate narratives. They are not listed in a chronological order.

Rabies in Jerusalem 1941

In 1941 a war was raging in Europe and in North Africa. On the whole Palestine was peaceful. Only occasional air raids by the Italian air force caused damage and some casualties in Haifa and once in Tel Aviv.

Jerusalem was quiet although the Jewish community was very concerned about the progress that the German army, under General Rommel, were making in their advance towards the Suez canal. The thought that the German army might cross the canal into Palestine filled us with horror. Our Arab friends and neighbours were rubbing their hands with joyful anticipation.

Of immediate daily concern was the announcement by the health authorities that rabies had appeared in the city of Jerusalem and its surroundings. Strict precautionary measures were recommended and publicised heavily.

Rabies is dreadful viral disease that causes inflammation of the brain and, if not treated urgently, is usually fatal. The rabies virus primarily infects mammals such as dogs and cats and gets transmitted to humans through bites, scratches or saliva from a diseased animal. The news caused alarm in the local population. All dogs were muzzled and many pets were kept at home to prevent them coming in contact with infected animals. The problem was that a stray dog might have been infected but showed no sign of being ill.

The situation affected my family in a very sad way. For a number of years I was the lucky owner of a gorgeous cat, which I named Mitzi. Mitzi was half white and half ginger. The ginger-red blotches dominated her personality so originally I was going to name her as Ginge. In fact through my love for Mitzi I developed a soft spot for ginger hair in humans.

Mitzi was a great companion and I would swear that she had a good sense of humour. She was very independent and strong-willed.

During the rabies panic we tried to stop her from leaving the flat. Alas, in spite of all the precautions Mitzi managed to get out and never came back. Just vanished.

I was heart-broken but my mother got literally hysterical.

My sister and I were subjected to ruthless third degree interrogations: 'Has Mitzi ever bitten you?' 'Has Mitzi ever scratched you?' 'Have you come in contact with Mitzi's spit?' My father, the doctor, was made to roam all the streets of the densely populated neighbourhood to search for Mitzi's body or find out if there were cases of rabies in the vicinity. He had to interview the local dustmen.

The trouble was that in case of a faint suspicion that Mitzi died of rabies and that either my sister or myself were bitten by a sick cat would have involved us in very painful and long series of injections to save our lives.

This trauma lasted a good few days. My mother aged in front of our eyes.

This hysteria came to an end when our friendly dustman arrived suddenly with a parcel containing Mitzi's body.

Now the drama started afresh.

'How did Mitzi die?' 'Was it rabies that killed her?' 'Should the kids be injected?'

I admired my father – he remained calm. He immediately took the dead body to the Government's laboratories and used his influence as an eminent doctor to ask for an urgent analysis of the cause of death of poor Mitzi. With all his influence and pleading it took a whole week to receive the results that announced that Mitzi did not die from rabies. What a relief for my mother. I remained very sad ever since. I still shed a tear or two when Mitzi's name is mentioned and I never had another pet cat or dog since.

An ancient water tunnel beneath the streets of Jerusalem.

Jerusalem water – gold dust

Visitors to Jerusalem who stay in any city hotel or with-friends can enjoy a bath or shower, drink tap water and watch the lovely green lawn outside being sprinkled for hours. The availability of water in such abundance is on par with any modern civilized city.

This abundant flow of water belies the historical dreadful shortage that pervaded life in Jerusalem over the millennia.

When King David occupied Jerusalem from the Jebusites (an off-shoot of the Canaanites) he discovered a couple of precious underground rivulets called Gihon and Pishon. During the summer months they were reduced to a trickle. However the population of Jerusalem after the occupation was so small that these two sources of water met the modest needs of the population. Baths and showers did not exist. An anecdotal legend purported that the stench from the great unwashed inside the city acted as a secret weapon against potential invaders. Apparently it took King David longer to occupy the city because of this 'weapon of mass malodorous stench'.

Casual visitors know little about the colossal number of projects, at times heroic, which were undertaken by umpteen enterprises over the years to enable the Jerusalem population to savour the experience of constant flow of water into every household in the town and its immediate surroundings.

Jerusalem is perched on arid hills with a very short rainy season. Between the end of February and November not a single drop of rain can be seen in Jerusalem.

Historically the locals had to dig a well with water-proof walls and catch into it the water during the rainy season. The content of the water accumulated in the well served the family needs throughout the summer months. The hygienic quality of the water trapped into these wells was pretty dubious.

The size of the water problem has grown with the expanding population of the city. During Jesus's time the population of Jerusalem was estimated to be 40,000. This figure included Roman troops.

Today the population is 875,000 and growing rapidly towards one million. Obviously the need for water has increased exponentially.

The British Mandated Government jointly with the Jewish Agency, the body representing the Jewish community at the time, built a 19-inch pipeline 60 kilometres in length, from the source of the Yarkon River near Petach Tikva.

The pipeline included a few powerful pumping stations that drove the water uphill to a height of 1500 metres. The water was stored into a reservoir that served Jerusalem's needs.

Unfortunately during the War of Independence in 1948, when Jerusalem was besieged by the Egyptian Army, Arab militias placed explosives in a number of locations and destroyed the pipeline. Jerusalem was left without regular supply of water.

The Jewish community launched a heroic regular donkey-drawn water tank service in the streets of Jerusalem. People queued for hours with pails and buckets to collect small quantities of water for urgent needs. Tragically the Egyptians continued to shell Jerusalem and quite a few citizens queuing for their meager share of the water perished during these bombardments. Two of our neighbors were caught by a shell and killed.

The water situation during the siege became alarming. A dramatic solution emerged with the incredible daring and determination of the Haganah to break the siege of Jerusalem by hurriedly building a road coupled with a pipeline a few miles away from the main battlefield. The road was given the name Burma Road in memory of a similar enterprise by the British Army in Burma during WWII.

This project was probably one of the most significant factors in changing the course of the war and promoting Israeli victory over the invading Arab armies. The siege was broken.

The infrastructural Jerusalem water problem has been tackled since then with remarkable creativity, enterprise and huge investment.

Israel's biggest water project since 1950 is now being tunneled under Jerusalem. A huge pipeline is meant to supply

Jerusalem and its suburbs with water for decades to come. It is one of Israel's biggest infrastructure projects. Altogether the way Israel engineered a country-wide network of canals, tunnels, aqueducts and aquifers to provide water to distant parts, including the Negev desert, is miraculous.

The word 'water' often pre-occupied our conversations and actions at home. My father, being a GP, was permanently concerned about the cleanliness of the water. He doubted whether water dragged uphill for 50 to 60 km could still be clean. He was aware of the frequent incidence of amoeba infection and para-typhoid among his patients.

I was subjected to endless taboos and prohibitions. Don't ever drink 'water from the tap'; 'Don't rinse your teeth with unboiled water'; 'When you visit friends only drink water from sealed bottles – make sure that the seal is unbroken'; 'Don't ever touch an ice-lolly'. This last edict was painful inasmuch as all my friends at school used to buy ice-lollies from the ice-cream vendor around the corner from the school. I felt a lonely 'odd-man-out'. While they were licking the ice-lolly with obvious pleasure I felt deprived of that pleasure. Clearly I have 'mega-fussy parents…' Every now and again the thought of rebelling against all these diktats crossed my mind. I watched all my friends enjoying the ice-lollies and none of them died from it or developed some nasty illness. I had pocket money and if I broke the rule once in a while nobody would be the wiser. I decided to assert my independence and cross the Rubicon…

One fine day I left school with all my mates and as a precaution I stood at the tail end of the queue. Exciting day. I was about to break family rules but savour the pleasure of licking an ice-lolly.

The queue moved quickly and with a shaking hand I gave my coin to the iceman and picked up my lolly. Heavens! I almost died on the spot. Who should arrive from around the corner? My sister Leah.

'What are you doing? Are you mad? You know the house rules!! Mother will kill you when she hears about it...'

I tried to employ all my creativity and imagination towards conjuring a plausible alibi but failed.

In desperation I dropped the lolly on the ice-box of the vendor and forgot about the money. Thus I both lost the money and the lolly. Floundering I said to Leah 'My friend Mossy asked me to buy this lolly for him...' 'Come on. You sodding liar. You are in big trouble. We'd better negotiate a deal for my silence'. A two page treaty was negotiated with many conditions. The top item confirmed again and again that I shall never seek to circumvent the rules of the house regarding hygiene in general and ice-pop lollies in particular. I never touched an ice-lolly since throughout my life.

Hayyim Nahman Bialik.

Bialik wished he never met me

My maternal grandmother, Rachel Rokach (Savta), lived at 43 Rothschild Boulevard, Tel Aviv. Uncle Itzhak and his family lived in a flat above.

A few times a year we took an Egged bus from Jerusalem to Tel Aviv to visit Savta. We stayed with her a few days and on a warm day we went to the beach for an immersion in the sea. This is where I started to learn to swim from an early age.

On one occasion during the summer of 1933 we got on the bus and suddenly mother uttered a whoop of delight 'Look who is on the bus with us: dear Mr. Bialik'. He responded with equal warmth 'Shalom my dear Hannah…' As a young kid I savoured the excitement of meeting a family friend although I did not know who Bialik was.

'This is my son Shimon, he is three and a half years old Shimon, say hello to Mr. Bialik'… Unbeknown to me Bialik was very friendly with the Rokach family and especially with Uncle Israel who was mayor of Tel Aviv. I did not realise at the time what a privilege it was to meet Haim Nachman Bialik who was recognised as the national poet of the Jewish community. In the UK he would earn the title of 'Poet Laureate'.

Together with Eliezer Ben Yehuda he is credited with the process of reviving the Hebrew language and morphing the biblical Hebrew into a modern living language.

'Come here my dear young man and sit in the lap of Uncle Haim'. Who could refuse such an invitation? The bus was crowded and I had the choice of either sitting in my mother's lap or Uncle Haim's lap. Moreover he called me 'young man'.

I was flattered. I felt like an adult.

The bus left in time with me being ensconced in the lap of the great national poet. I was overwhelmed with excitement.

The suspension of the Egged buses at the time was rather rickety with the result that I was being tossed up and down steadily in my host's lap. The inevitable happened: my bladder's retention system gave up and I peed into the lap of our illustrious national poet.

The so called 'dear young man' was tossed unceremoniously on the floor with a shriek of consternation. My mother joined in the melee and showered me with the biggest admonitory tirade that a three year old ever heard. She went on and on mercilessly as if I peed on purpose.

The victim of my flood expressed a poetic tongue lashing that was above my head but sounded very angry. He kept looking at the little puddle on the floor with great distaste.

My mother fussed with her favourite shawl trying to wipe the liquid from his lap. This made Bialik even angrier.

Israel Rokach, Mayor of Tel Aviv.

I never recovered from this episode. Tragically Bialik passed away in Vienna in 1934. I needed frequent reassurance that my peeing in his lap was not a contributory factor for his early death.

The other resolution I made was never to invite a three-year-old to sit on my lap in a rickety bus.

Arturo Toscanini.

Huberman and Toscanini

Arturo Toscanini, considered one of the finest virtuoso conductors of the 20th century, was conducting the New York Philharmonic Symphony Orchestra in 1935 when he was approached by Bronislaw Huberman and asked to conduct the opening performance of the Palestine Philharmonic.

Huberman, a violinist, had been recruiting Jewish musicians to form the Palestine Philharmonic from among those who had been dismissed from their positions in Germany and Austria for being Jewish after the Nazis rose to power. Huberman always found the process of selecting the finest performers and turning down the rest a most painful experience. He felt that by selecting the best he was possibly passing a death sentence on the others. Toscanini's agreement to conduct the opening session helped attract even more musicians to the new enterprise. Altogether the new orchestra consisted of outstanding musicians from many countries.

Toscanini was a noted opponent of fascism and the Nazi Party. In 1933, he had refused to participate in a festival in

Bronislaw Huberman.

Bayreuth as a protest against the Nazi regime and had been honoured by Jewish community leaders in New York and by the Jewish National Fund for his public stance. He refused to take payment or reimbursement for his travel saying, 'I had to show my solidarity. It is everyone's duty to help in this cause according to one's means.'

Toscanini arrived at the Lod airport at approximately noon on 20 December 1936 where he was received by Huberman and Chaim Weizmann, among other dignitaries. After arriving, he was taken immediately to the concert hall to rehearse with the orchestra. Toscanini would conduct the orchestra in its first concert on December 26, 1936 to a sold-out crowd of 3,000.

In addition to his time with the orchestra, the renowned conductor also spent time touring the country and meeting Jewish refugees and immigrants from Europe. He even participated in a tree planting ceremony. He returned to Palestine in 1938 during the height of the Arab riots and again conducted a series of concerts with the Palestine Philharmonic.

My mother's sister Miriam Rokach-Katz (known to us as Doda Miriam) was a founder-member together with Huberman of the whole project. Her main task was to welcome the illustrious visiting conductors and soloists who came from abroad and attend to their needs. Toscanini lodged in her apartment during his various visits. She travelled with the orchestra on all their major tours.

To my great pleasure and good luck whenever the orchestra came to perform in Jerusalem, Doda Miriam included me among the select invitees. Thus at the age of nine I was privileged to rub shoulders with the leaders of the Jewish community in Jerusalem as well as eminent conductors and soloists. At the time I was not aware how lucky I was to shake the hands of

Toscanini and Huberman. I found them both very charming and they chatted with me in a most non-patronising way.

One of the orchestra's visits to Jerusalem left an unforgettable impact on me. It was probably the watershed occasion when, at the age of nine I became aware of the true beauty of music and it became an integral part of my character and long-term field of interest. The concert in question took place in the open-air amphitheatre attached to the Hebrew University campus.

The amphitheatre is perched on top of the hill called Mount Scopus. It faces east and on a clear day you can see at the distance the Moab Hills (in Jordan) and the Dead Sea. The view is breathtaking. At the distance you can see an array of small Arab villages and on the slopes flocks of sheep complete the sublime pastoral scenery.

The amphitheatre itself consists of continuous circular stone rows providing simple stone seats. At the age of 9 I found the seating arrangement most appealing although I noticed that many people in the audience brought cushions with them.

The concert itself was enchanting. The orchestra started with the Beethoven violin concerto with Bronislaw Huberman performing the solo part. Doda Miriam, who sat next to me, nudged me and whispered in my ear 'watch the violin – it is a famous Stradivarius'. I little knew what that meant but I stored this bit of information and quizzed her later about it.

The main piece was Beethoven's Symphony No. 6, the 'Pastoral'. Listening to the 'Pastoral' in the midst of the most glorious environment is a memorable experience. I kept looking at the flocks of sheep scattered around the hills and felt that the music was written for them. I wondered if they could hear the music and enjoy it as much as I did. The 'Pastoral' became my favourite symphony and whenever I hear it I am catapulted mentally to that glorious scene in Mount Scopus with Toscanini conducting the Palestine Philharmonic.

The name Stradivarius stuck in my mind and with hindsight it is when my interest in lutherie was triggered, culminating scores of years later in my decision to make violins.

Huberman's Stradivarius depicts a fascinating history that spawned umpteen dramatic programmes on television and radio including a number of films.

Huberman's Strad started its history as the Gibson Stradivarius. It was fabricated in Cremona by Stradivarius in 1713 and first owned by George Alfred Gibson, the famous English violinist. The name Gibson followed it regardless of who owned subsequently. For a while it was owned and played on by Norbert Brainin, the first violin of the Amadeus Quartet.

When Huberman acquired this violin its appellation was changed to Huberman-Gibson Stradivarius and remained so ever since.

The Huberman-Gibson underwent the most dramatic episodes of theft. In 1919 the violin was stolen from Huberman's Hotel room in Vienna. Luckily it was recovered within a short time.

Shortly after a visit to Palestine Huberman was performing at Carnegie Hall. During the interval the Strad was stolen from his dressing room. All the attempts to locate it and the perpetrators of the theft failed. The violin remained at large, its whereabouts unknown, for nearly 50 years. Tragically Huberman died in Switzerland in 1947 and was never re-united with his beloved Stradivarius-Gibson.

In 1985 an unremarkable New York violinist named Julian Altman made a deathbed confession to his wife. He told her that he had purchased the violin for $100 although speculation remains that he himself was the thief. A most extraordinary chain of events followed. The violin was recovered by the Lloyds Insurance and for a while was played on by Norbert Brainin. Ultimately was acquired for a vast amount of money by Joshua Bell, the famous violinist who still owns it.

I was very lucky to have heard this remarkable violin played by Bronislaw Huberman, Norbert Brainin and Joshua Bell – three brilliant virtuosos.

Living opposite a Yeshiva

My parents decided to move from their spacious apartment in the hospital in the Old City following the dreadful massacre in Hebron in 1929. The location of the hospital in the midst of a hostile environment was very vulnerable.

The modern quarters in the newer parts of the west of the city felt distinctly safer inasmuch very few Arabs lived in those areas. Moreover in the newer districts the Jewish community established well-trained defence units.

While my parents decided to move their home away from the Old City the hospital with all its patients remained behind. My father remained in charge and needed to attend for his normal duties plus his GP practice every day. This meant that he needed to walk or travel every day from the safe part of Jerusalem to the less safe one. For many years it caused us all great anxiety. On many occasions in later years I remember the fear I harboured, when my father went to work in the Old City, that I may not see him again – a painful experience for a young boy.

In search of a suitable accommodation my parents looked for an area in which the demography was suitable for my father's medical practice. We moved from apartment to apartment until we settled in a flat with a garden in a street called Sfat Emet, meaning 'language of truth'. The name was given to the street because across the road from our flat it housed a very famous Yeshiva by that name. The Yeshiva was founded by the illustrious Hassidic 'Gerrer Rebbe' (Grand Rabbi Abraham Mordechai Alter, originally from the Ukraine).

Living opposite a Yeshiva in a narrow street creates a few problems. The main one is the fact that this Yeshiva was housed in a fairly small building without suitable space for leisure or networking. During break times they all drifted into the road. Around 100 Hassidic students, all dressed in black, talking at the top of their voices, is an intimidating falanx of religious fanatics. Moreover I had to avoid them because walking in short sleeves without a hat I was glared at by them collectively as an undesirable virus. I solved the problem by not going out of our flat or coming back during the Yeshiva breaks, which were fortunately happening at regular time.

My sister Leah, on the other hand, was on a war footing with these zealots. Owing to the fact that my father was a doctor we were the happy possessors of a telephone. A number of Yeshiva students had the Chutzpah of giving our number to their friends and relatives. It became a major nuisance.

The phone rings. 'Can you ask Moishe from the Yeshiva across the road to take this call?' No please, no apology, just go and get Moishe. Our phone became a public one. At one stage Leah wanted to be charitable and helpful. She would cross the road with the falanx of students in black jabbering. As she approached this mob they all turned round displaying their backs and tzizes. It is verboten to look at a very attractive young lady in bare arms and some décolleté. 'A phone call for Moishe,' she declares. She is ignored. 'A phone call for Moishe' she repeats in angry voice. Ignored again. She storms back to our flat and tells the caller, 'Sorry there is no Moishe in the Yeshiva' and puts the receiver down. The minute she cuts the line a knock at our door and a young man announces 'I am Moishe, where is the phone?'

'This phone is only available for polite people. None of your friends are…Goodbye'. Moishe is ejected from our flat.

After that Leah had fun creating umpteen tricks to obstruct callers for the Yeshiva students and refusing to cross the road. She planned a methodical and ruthless campaign of teaching the ' Yeshiva-bochers' some manners. One day she came home jubilant: 'the Yeshiva students gave me a smile. I wish I had a camera with me… The 'Gerrer Rebbe' would have turned in his grave!'

Grotte aux pigeons, Beirut.

Escape to the Lebanon

The years 1936-1939 were a very troubled period in the history of the British mandatory control of Palestine.

The Arabs in Palestine were led by the so-called Arab Higher Committee, presided over by the militant Jerusalem Mufti Haj Amin Al-Husseini, who already in the early 1920s was an ardent supporter of Hitler and the Nazis. He refused to negotiate at any stage with the Jewish leadership and was a rabid anti-Semite. His mission, allegedly, was often described in the following message to his adherents:

'Arise, o sons of Arabia. Fight for your sacred rights. Slaughter Jews wherever you find them. Their spilled blood pleases Allah, our history and religion. That will save our honour.'

Haj Amin instigated what became known as the 'Arab Revolt' or known in the Jewish community as 'the Troubles'. Strikes, rioting and random killing of Jews throughout the country became daily occurrence. Many areas in the country in which Jews and Arabs lived in close proximity became unsafe. Many properties including orchards and citrus groves were vandalised

Left: The Mufti of Jerusalem, Haj Amin Al-Husseini, leader of the Arab Revolt. *Right:* British Major-General Orde Wingate.

or destroyed. The main goal of the revolt was a demand to stop Jewish immigration resulting from the rise of Nazism in Germany. Clearly this mass immigration was changing the demography of Palestine in favour of the Jewish community and the Arab Higher Committee wanted it stopped by legislation. The other major goal was a legal ban on Arab land sold to Jews. Altogether the Arabs wanted the British authorities to freeze the size of the Jewish population and prohibit acquisition of land by Jews. Haj Amin also demanded the right to establish an independent Arab national government.

All these demands were in direct conflict with the many promises made to the Jewish leadership including the Balfour Declaration. It needed the wisdom of King Solomon to unravel this impasse. In desperation the British policy makers appointed the Peel Commission to investigate the whole subject and suggest a solution. The Peel Commission recommended in 1937 the partition of Palestine into two states, one Arab and one Jewish, with the British retaining mandate control of Jerusalem and a few other cities. No proposal on actual borders was made.

The Peel Report was an amalgam of muddled thinking and a formula for potential endless conflicts. Nonetheless reluctantly the Zionist Congress accepted it as a basis for negotiations. Typically, the Arab Higher Committee rejected it out of hand and declared a full resumption of the Arab Revolt, but this time aimed also at the British military and police.

On reflection it is interesting to note that the reaction of the two sides (Arab and Jews) to strategic solutions to the impasse have not changed one iota since then. One side accepts, the other rejects. The same happened in 1947 in response to the much better UN partition plan.

Following the Arab rejection of the Peel Commission recommendation the revolt resumed in autumn of 1937. At this stage the British forces, supported by 6,000 armed Jewish defence units, fought the insurgents with overwhelming force.

The British Bible-lover General Charles Orde Wingate, loved by the Jewish community for his almost messianic dream of seeing a Jewish state born in the holy land, took command of the campaign.

Wingate organised Special Night Squads (SNS), composed of British soldiers and Jewish members of the Haganah, to undertake night raids on Arab villages and known hideouts. With ruthless, well-organised attacks these squads scored significant successes against the Arab rebels. Under Wingate's command and his strategy the Arab revolt gradually fizzled out. By the time the revolt concluded in March 1939, more than 5,000 Arabs, 400 Jews, and 200 British had been killed and at least 15,000 Arabs were wounded.

The attacks on the Jewish population by Arabs during the Troubles had the major result that a very effective Jewish defence system improved, primarily by the Haganah. The experience gained during these difficult years proved decisive in 1948 during the war of independence when the newly-born Israel had to fight all its invading Arab neighbours.

A far less helpful result of the Arab Revolt was a new British policy enshrined in a White Paper of 1939 intended to placate the Arabs. The White Paper restricted Jewish land purchase and Jewish immigration. This perverse U-turn soothed Arab opinion but was anathema to the Jewish side and created a serious chasm between the Jewish community and the British authorities, a chasm that did not heal until the British left Palestine in 1948.

During the Troubles life in Jerusalem was fairly unsafe, especially in the areas where the demography was mixed. Every day one heard of one or two attempts at assassination by shooting a Jewish passer-by. We were very unhappy about my father going every day to his hospital in the Old City. On the other hand people in Tel Aviv felt safe as long as they avoided walking into the more hostile Jaffa and its immediate Arab surroundings.

The consequence of all these safety problems was that during the summer holiday period people sought to escape to safer places. The rich planned holidays somewhere in Europe, especially in Switzerland where they felt perfectly safe. The less affluent took holidays in areas like Tel Aviv or other locations where the population was predominantly Jewish.

My parents were advised that the Lebanon was a good location for a safe and enjoyable holiday.

Our brief research confirmed that it was a lovely location and perfectly safe from the Arab Revolt. A decision was taken to plan an escape to the Lebanon for our vacations. The strategy worked brilliantly for three years until 1939.

On advice from good friends who knew the Lebanon intimately, my parents reserved rooms in a holiday hotel by the name of Medawar Hotel in a small village called Dhour El Choueir.

The village was inhabited in the main by Francophile Christian Maronites with the result that French was a dominant language in the area. My parents found this bit of information reassuring. The Lebanon was controlled at the time by the French, under a League of Nations Mandate, similar to the British Mandate in Palestine. The French influence at the time was more conspicuous in the Lebanon than the British presence in Palestine. The policemen in Beirut wore French-style kepis.

Dhour El Choueir.

Dhour El Choueir was a lovely village perched at an altitude of 1200 metres on a hill in the central Lebanese mountain massif. It was only 12 km from the coast and the view of Beirut and its surrounding from the village was breathtaking.

Not surprisingly Dhour El Choueir and neighbouring hamlets were very popular summer resorts for Beirut residents who wanted to escape from the stifling heat of the capital during the summer. Many well-off families had second homes in that area. In 30 minutes they could leave Beirut and be in their summer house in a glorious area surrounded by pine trees with awe-inspiring panorama.

A decision to go to Dhour El Choueir was taken and a hotel was booked after a brief correspondence. However, there was a major challenge: how do we get there safely?

Sister Leah, Uncle Israel Rokach (the Mayor of Tel Aviv), Simon and Mother.

The obvious way was to take a taxi from Jerusalem to Beirut, stay one night in Beirut and proceed the next day by taxi on a short journey to Dhour El Choueir. Jewish taxi drivers refused to do this journey because it involved driving through very hostile Arab area, especially in North Galilee. Arab taxi drivers were happy to do the journey but we were unable to verify their credentials of reliability and peaceful intents.

The idea of boarding a ship that sails from Tel Aviv-Jaffa to Beirut was recommended by friends who had used this mode of transport while avoiding the dangerous coast road to Beirut. My parents discovered that an Italian maritime shipping company Lloyd Triestino ran a regular service from Trieste via Jaffa and Haifa to Beirut and then to Turkey.

I was very excited. This was the first time that I was travelling 'abroad'. Starting the holiday with a cruise, albeit for one night, was the icing on the cake.

My mother, sister Leah and myself were honoured to be escorted to the Jaffa Harbour by Uncle Israel Rokach, the Mayor of Tel Aviv.

Neither Tel-Aviv nor Jaffa had docking jetty facilities at the time. The ship was anchored a few hundred metres away from the harbour and passengers were ferried in special launches. I shall never forget the excitement of approaching a beautiful large ship in a small launch. We all climbed a fairly steep gangway to be met by smart uniformed Italian stewards. I was only sad that this part of the holiday was for one night only. The luxury around the boat, the beautiful cabin given to us for one night and the catering were dazzling for my sister Leah, aged 11, and me, aged 8. We were not accustomed to such opulence.

The boat left late at night and proceeded to Haifa where it anchored for a couple of hours to unload some cargo and allowing passengers to embark and disembark.

The next stop in the morning was Beirut. Beirut at the time had a proper wharf so we could disembark by a gangway straight to terra firma.

The plan was to spend one night in Beirut but we did not have a hotel reservation. We were assured that Beirut had many cheap hotels. With all our luggage we marched in search of a hotel. There were many small hotels and after a brief haggling about the price for one night a hotel was selected. I do not remember much about the hotel and its immediate surroundings.

We had glimpse of the most amazing natural rock formation known as the Grotte aux Pigeons – probably the most impressive natural monument in Beirut.

Other than the remarkable Grotte aux Pigeons our short stay in Beirut was uneventful. The one thing I do remember vividly and with some revulsion is that all our beds in the hotel were infested with bed bugs. It dampened our enthusiasm for Beirut for a while.

A half-hour taxi ride on the Beirut-Damascus road brought us to Dhour El Choueir towards a glorious holiday in beautiful surroundings and fresh air.

Dhour El Choueir was one of a few typical Lebanese villages of pre-war popular resorts located in the middle of beautiful pine forests. In Dhour El Choueir, the charm of the place was manifested by beautiful buildings of the twentieth century, restaurants, lively cafés and a breathtaking view of the majestic Mount Sannine on one side and the Mediterranean Sea and Beirut on the other side. The Medawar Hotel was charming and most welcoming. It had beautiful gardens, swimming pool, excellent restaurant and well-equipped playground with tennis court, mini-golf and croquet. It proved to be perfect for our needs. My mother was delighted with all the arrangements and the great view from our room's balcony. 'This is so much like Switzerland and the Alps' she announced. She was educated in the Lausanne Conservatoire and lived there for three years and was therefore able to draw this parallel.

On three evenings every week the hotel sponsored concerts, mostly solo piano or lieder programmes. These were formal occasions and most guests came attired in formal outfits. The whole atmosphere was very European rather than Middle Eastern. Most of the guests were French speakers.

We thoroughly enjoyed our stay in this hotel. Leah and I managed to make many friends among the younger guests. We spent many happy hours playing all sorts of games with them. Once a week the hotel organised a delightful display of fireworks followed by a dance with a band and refreshments. Many of the children including us joined in the dancing and were encouraged to do so. At the age of eight I mastered (badly) the steps of waltz, foxtrot and tango.

We used the hotel as our base and periodically rented a taxi to take us on day trips to interesting locations round the country. We visited many villages and monuments of ancient origin. Two places left an unforgettable impact on me: Baalbek and Cedars of Lebanon. Both places are mentioned in the Bible in two different contexts.

Baalbek is an incredible monument, standing on a hill in the Beqaa valley in Lebanon. The construction of the temple started by the Phoenicians between three and four thousand years ago. The Greeks then added to it, followed by the Romans, and much later the Arabs. The size of this

Baalbek.

extensive temple is overpowering. Baal is one of the pagan gods mentioned in the Bible. Baalbek therefore means the 'City of God' – pagan god.

In order to see the Cedars of Lebanon in their awe-inspiring glory we stayed for a couple of days in a lovely town called Ehden. This town is an extraordinary ski resort in the winter and spring and a popular resort in the summer for the horde of visitors who come to see the famous cedars of Lebanon in their natural habitat.

The ski season in the Cedar area is similar to the Alps, typically runs from mid-December to April, depending on the length and depth of snowfall. In spring, it is sometimes possible to snow ski in the morning and drive to the coast in the afternoon to water ski.

A magnificent Cedar of Lebanon.

The cedar of Lebanon is a species of tree in the pine family Pinaceae, native to the mountains of the Eastern Mediterranean basin. It is an evergreen conifer that can reach 40 m (130 ft) in height.

Cedar trees are protected nowadays with great care and belong to rigorous control under National Park regulations, but it is sad to be told that in the distant past the whole central Lebanese mountain range was covered by these beautiful trees. Many of those currently in existence are over 1000 years old. The wood from these trees is remarkably durable and resistant to the elements.

The Phoenicians, Egyptians, Assyrians, Babylonians and Persians used the cedar wood for shipbuilding. The Ottoman Empire, which controlled the Lebanon for centuries, cut down many trees for laying railway sleepers. Much earlier King Solomon acquired large quantities of cedar wood for building his temple in Jerusalem.

What one can see today of this glorious tree is a fraction of the past rich forest that covered miles of the mountain slopes.

The visit to the Cedars of Lebanon region left a very deep impression on all of us but we were also sad to realise that these trees are running the risk of extinction over the forthcoming years in spite of all the attempts to protect them.

We were having lovely holidays in the Lebanon. The air was fresh, the scenery beautiful, the hotel remarkably enjoyable and accommodating. Only one emotional cloud undermined our general contentment in the paradisaical setting of Dhohr El Choueir.

Our plan was to enjoy a holiday en famille for 6-8 weeks. However my father was only able to stay with us for two weeks. He insisted on returning to his duty as the doctor in charge of the hospital in the Old City and his busy GP practice. This happened on every occasion during our stays in the Lebanon.

This decision raised alarm bells: Father back in Jerusalem and having to cross the Jaffa Gate every day was a daunting prospect. Jaffa Gate was notorious for its random shooting by snipers. The three of us pleaded with him to stay overnight in the flat in the hospital to avoid having to cross the dangerous Jaffa Gate every day. He promised to do so but none of the three of us believed that our intrepid father would obey this request. He was fearless.

The only bit of good news we heard was that by communicating with his many Arab patients he discovered that one of them, a taxi driver, whom he knew well as a patient, was prepared to come all the way to Dhour El Choueir and pick him up for the whole journey. This driver, Abu Yossef, became our regular transporter for all our future journeys to and from the Lebanon without having to stop in a bed-bug infested hotel in Beirut or resort to a boat trip from Jaffa to Beirut.

We knew that Abu Yossef was safe and loyal. He revered my father and we felt more confident that he was in safe hands. With the help of Abu Yossef our logistics became well-organised. Father joined us from time to time and we knew that we had a reliable transporter for future journeys.

The first two holidays in 1937 and 1938 were most enjoyable and trouble-free.

The last trip to the Lebanon in 1939 was a bit fraught and we were caught in the general anxiety about the political situation in Europe and the likelihood of a war with Germany. As children we did not appreciate the full meaning of the situation but every conversation in the hotel sooner or later involved the words war, Chamberlain, Czechoslovakia and Poland. My mother became very anxious and dreaded the idea of being stuck in Dhour El Choueir when a war is declared. After long consultations with my father and other good friends a decision was taken to cut the holiday short by one month and return home. A few weeks after our return home Germany invaded Poland and World War Two was declared.

Altogether our vacations in the Lebanon were truly enjoyable, wholesome and memorable. Sadly the political developments in the Middle East precluded us from visiting this lovely country again.

Tragically Dhour El Choueir got caught in horrendous Lebanese civil war lasting from 1975 to 1990 which resulted on an estimated 120,000 fatalities. The war resulted in an exodus of almost one million people, mostly the Christian Maronites, from the Lebanon.

The Lebanon population consisted of an amalgam of Shias, Sunnis, Christians, Maronite Christians, Druzes, Palestinian refugees and Hezbollah, all seeking dominance in a small country. A so-called Hotel War started in Beirut and other cities. Each hotel was taken over by one militia or another and relentless shooting and bombing against each other inflicted huge damage all round.

Dhour El Choueir did not escape this calamity. Many of the larger hotels got caught in the Hotel War and were destroyed and abandoned. The town suffered serious damage. My research seems to suggest that considerable re-building has taken place. I suspect that the demography of the town has changed dramatically and therefore the character of the town is not the same.

My sister and I derived enormous social and cultural benefits from the series of Lebanon holidays. It represented a milestone in our education and development. As a special bonus our spoken French improved and I learnt to tango.

Golda Meir.

Golda

The so-called British Mandate in Palestine was a hybrid concept invented by the League of Nations seeking to avoid designating the country as a colony.

The main aim of the League's mandate system was to administer parts of the defunct Ottoman Empire, which had been in control of the Middle East since the 16th century, until such time as these territories were able to stand alone.

A Palestine government and administration were set up by the British authorities to mirror the style and modus operandi of the system that existed in the UK.

Instead of ministries the administration consisted of departments. The civil service represented an amalgam of experienced British civil servants who moved to live in Palestine plus Jews, Arabs and Christians well educated individuals with experience in public administration. The system evolved into a fairly sleek and well-managed administration.

Jerusalem was the capital and most government transactions were conducted in English.

High Commissioner Sir Herbert Samuel.

The head of the government was a High Commissioner, appointed by the Crown in London. The High Commissioner resided in a palatial mansion on the outskirts of Jerusalem, known as Government House.

The first High Commissioner appointed shortly after Palestine was occupied by the British under General Allenby was Sir Herbert Samuel, a Jew. Herbert Samuel's appointment was a serious mistake on the part of the British Colonial Office. He was a lovely person but the fact that he was Jewish

High Commissioner Viscount Gort.

opened a can of worms. The Arab community were outraged that Palestine under the British control was to be run by a Jew. Samuel tried to over-compensate and to be impartial at all times but by doing so he managed to upset the Jewish side of the equation. It was a no-win situation.

After Herbert Samuel none of the subsequent appointees were Jewish. A few of them were well-known retired Generals. Their individual relationship with the local communities varied between very popular and highly disliked.

The most popular was Field Marshall Viscount Gort, a hero of WWI fame who had received the Victoria Cross, Britain's highest award for gallantry. The week he arrived in Jerusalem he insisted on attending a concert of the Palestine Philharmonic Orchestra in the Edison Cinema. He was met with a warm applause. He arrived without any noticeable bodyguard and sat in the centre stalls surrounded by a normal audience. Alas, he only lasted one year and had to return the UK for medical reasons. We were very disappointed.

A tradition emerged for the High Commissioners to hold periodic 'audiences' with political leaders of the local communities. These 'audiences' were modelled on the one practiced in London when the monarch holds regular meetings with whoever was the PM at the time.

Here it was more complicated because these meetings had to be arranged with maximum diplomacy in inviting leaders of communities at constant state of dissonance.

My mother's brother, Israel Rokach, was a frequent invitee to these audience meetings with the High Commissioner. As the Mayor of Tel Aviv, the largest city in Palestine, he was an obvious candidate.

Whenever he came to Jerusalem for these meetings he always stopped at our modest flat to greet us. I was always impressed by this manifestation of devoted family cordiality.

For my part I had a glimmer of a suspicion that in addition to family love he had two mini ulterior motives. He knew that on arrival at our domain a large bowl of pistachio and cashew nuts would wait for him. Israel was forbidden from eating nuts at home. His dear wife Esther declared them to be poisonous and dangerous to health. Eureka! Once in a while, in Jerusalem, he had a 'nuts holiday' for which he was most grateful. He used to guzzle the content of the bowl in supersonic speed.

The other item which became a routine procedure as part of the brief visit was asking my father, the doctor, to take his blood-pressure and discuss the implications. So nuts and blood pressure became a preamble to meeting the state supremo, the High Commissioner.

Meanwhile his limousine, chauffeur and bodyguard blocked our narrow road and created great curiosity among the neighbours and the Yeshiva inmates.

Once in a while Uncle Israel arrived escorted by some other significant political leader. He brought them in and they were offered tea, coffee and nuts (if any were left). We did not always know who these casual visitors were, although we suspected that that they were important personalities in their own political milieu. One day Uncle Israel arrived with a very severe looking lady in a long black skirt. He introduced her as Golda. We did not catch her surname. She was in some hurry to go to our loo.

We were comfortably settled in the living room when suddenly we heard what sounded like a mini-explosion. We were mystified by what our guest was doing in our loo. She emerged a short while later, walked towards the living room sat down and did not say a word. The only time she addressed me was to ask which school I was attending. I detected an American accent.

The party left about ten minutes later. Nuts were devoured; blood-pressure had been taken and deliberated upon and Golda's mini-explosion remained a mystery.

Following their departure we ventured into our toilet to undertake some detective work to discover the cause of the mysterious bang. The answer stared us in the face: Golda, with her weight, managed to smash our rather fragile wooden toilet seat into fragments. Yet she said nothing on emerging out of the bathroom.

Much to our surprise a week later we received a generous cheque from my Uncle Israel to pay for a new seat. Golda had confided to him of the incident.

Later we discovered who Golda was. It was a great honour to meet her in spite of the most unexpected circumstances. At that point she was a senior Labour party politician, a good public speaker with a very promising career ahead.

Golda Meir (1898–1978) was the fourth Prime Minister of Israel, in office between 1969 and 1974. She is the only woman to have served as Israeli Prime Minister. Golda Meir has become known for her bluntness, strong will and determination. She started life as a teacher, hence the one question about which school I was attending. At one stage she was Israel's ambassador to the Soviet Union.

I shall never forget her.

Hamor Shalem

Shalem in Hebrew means 'total' or 'complete'. In certain circumstances the Hebrew meaning, as we shall see later, came to haunt Mr. Shalem, our geography and science teacher.

His approach was biblical inasmuch as for every new scientific concept he extracted suitable evidence from the Old Testament. 'Nothing is new in our world'.

Among my friends we had standard joke about Shalem: 'why did it take Moses 40 years to cross the Sinai desert when it could be done in days'? Answer: because he used Mr. Shalem as his guide'... Ah, Ah, Ah. On the whole Shalem was out-of-touch with the younger generations and to that extent was vulnerable to tricks that they inflicted upon him

Shalem had a few obsessions . One of them related to his love for donkeys. He asserted that the donkey is the loveliest animal in our universe. He claimed that the donkey is intelligent, hard-working, loyal, he even felt that the donkey has a sense of humour. He used to tell jokes to donkeys and swore that he could see a smile in response. He admitted that sometimes a donkey could be stubborn but averred that when a donkey behaves in a stubborn way it only did it with a good reason.

Donkey in Hebrew is hamor. When an Israeli talks about hamor it is usually pejorative. To call someone a hamor is a real insult. Yet Shalem loved this animal and defended its important role in the world.

Moreover being a biblical scholar Shalem discovered that the name Hamor existed in the bible.

Who was Hamor in the Bible (Genesis)? Hamor was the leader of the Hivites whose centre was a town called Shechem. In later years Shechem became the capital of Samaria. Nowadays it is a significant city in the West Bank of Palestine and is called Nablus.

The Hivites were one of the tribes that originated from the people of Canaan that had populated that part of the country when Abraham settled there. Abraham's grandson, Jacob, was eager to initiate a policy of commercial and social relationship with his Hivite neighbours. It was even suggested that Jacob's daughter Dinah might marry Shechem, the son of Hamor (the same name as the town).

Sadly this attempt at some alliance ended in a tragedy. During an informal encounter between Schechem and Dinah she was abused and raped. Her two brothers Simeon and Levi, Jacob's sons, took violent revenge. They raised an army and attacked the Hivite's capital and killed a large number of its male population. This put an end to the rapprochement between Jacob's Hebrew tribe and the Hivites.

So the name Hamor existed in the Old Testament. For Mr. Shalem this was a clincher. He decided that it was a respectable name to give to a baby. Moreover it was redolent of his beloved donkey.

The rumour that followed stuck to Mr. Shalem like a carbuncle.

The story spread that his wife had a baby son and Shalem decided to call him Hamor Shalem. Alas as we saw earlier Shalem means total. So Hamor Shalem means Total Ass. The birth certificate registrar objected but on hearing that Hamor existed in the Bible withdrew his objection. The finale, according to the enthusiastic story-tellers in our midst, was that Mrs. Shalem left her husband wishing him a long life with his donkeys. Since then nobody chose the name Hamor for their son.

The second major obsession of Mr. Shalem and the consequences will follow. In this case SM's role was significant and shameful.

Hills in the Judean Desert.
Photograph by David Shankbone.

The glistening pebble

Mr Shalem taught us Geography and Science. His approach to the two subjects was idiosyncratic and too dependent on biblical sources. He was of the opinion that all scientific phenomena existed before and recorded in the Bible.

If he were alive today (I presume that he is not – otherwise he would be more than 120 – a good biblical age...) he would aver that climate change started with Noah, who saved the world by building his famous ark that accommodated one couple of every species on earth.

In common with other scientists he believed in the theory that millions of years ago Jerusalem and the Judean hills were covered by water as part of the Mediterranean Sea. The problem is how to prove it.

Mr. Shalem postulated that if sea water was covering the whole area with constant movement due to tides or grating waves the resulting abrasion over the millennia would have caused the pebbles and stones near the surface to develop a luminous sheen reminiscent of a glass marble. If such shiny pebbles could be found it would have presented a strong case in support of Mr. Shalem's theory.

We, the pupils in the Science Stream, about 20 of us, were given the task of locating 'shiny pebbles' in the Judean Hills outside Jerusalem.

At the beginning we found the project quite exciting. Going for long walks in the hills, outside Jerusalem, equipped with trowels and sieves, digging for shining pebbles, sounded like fun. It was a relief from being cooped up in a classroom.

After a while, however, these excursions became tedious and fruitless. We dug the earth's surface for hours. We sieved mountains of earth. We located oodles of pebbles but none bore the slightest sign of sheen. The most promising discovery was what looked like the remains of a shiny marble, soon discovered to be a shard from a broken Coca Cola bottle. The level of frustration was climbing to a state of fastigium.

'Don't worry. Next time we shall have more luck'. It dawned on us that to prove scientific theory you need luck. We were praying that luck would come soon.

Shortly after the last 'shiny pebble-hunting excursion' came the Pesach (Passover) break for a couple of weeks. For many years my family had the tradition of moving to a lovely hotel in Tiberias by the lake to celebrate Pesach. I loved those family holidays. Although the lake was very cold I enjoyed swimming in it. On one occasion coming out of the water my eye caught a few shiny pebbles. WOW! I picked up one of the glistening ones and placed it in my swim-trunks pocket.

Sadly the pebble was found in Tiberias and not in Jerusalem. Yet who would know?...

A couple of months elapsed before the next 'pebble-hunting' was due to take place. Meanwhile I cherished my serendipitous find with love and great sense of achievement. My logic was telling me that Jerusalem and Tiberias are not that far apart in the context of the world space. If Jerusalem was under water millions of years ago probably so was Tiberias.

So I was in possession of a most dramatic evidence in support of Mr. Shalem's scientific obsession.

I waited patiently for the next 'shining pebble' search party. It arrived on a lovely warm summer day. We became very skilful at digging, sieving and messing about. We were also getting thoroughly bored with the whole project.

The big moment arrived when I plucked my Tiberias glimmering pebble out of my pocket and exclaimed with great enthusiasm: 'Mr. Shalem, look what I have just found'! The collective accolade and standing ovation could probably be heard in Tiberias, where the stone furtively arrived from.

The general excitement was palpable. Mr. Shalem had his famous theory validated. He was in high heaven. He was longing to having this 'achievement' enhancing his standing among the fraternity of scientists.

Our group felt that the chore of digging for glistening pebbles is coming to an end. The mission has been completed with great success. On my part I put aside my qualms about being a cheat and savoured my new hero-status about to unfold.

Shortly afterwards Mr. Shalem issued a brief newsletter summarising the whole story with my contribution eulogised in glowing terms. I was getting more and more embarrassed by the fake tour de force that I unleashed. I was guilt-ridden.

My real big problem emerged when my sister Leah, who attended the same school, three years ahead of me, saw the notice and realised immediately what her crazy brother had done.

'You can't allow this story to go on. You are interfering with serious scientific research. This is insane what you have done. You must go to Mr. Shalem and apologise and tell him the truth. If you don't I will.'

I was trapped. I could not sleep for nights and dreaded the consequences of my folly. Eventually I surrendered to my sister's ultimatum and went to see Mr. Shalem and confessed with tears in my eyes and burning red face coupled with a blizzard of absurd excuses. My fall from grace was reported in the next newsletter. My image of the metamorphosis from hero status to a mini fraudster followed me for quite a while. The one consolation was that my class-mates admired my creative scam that put an end to the futile excursions to the Judean hills in search of shiny pebbles. At least my own peers were on my side.

Teacher EK

My class at the Gymnasia High School in 1942 was a very boisterous one. Out of 50 kids around 30 were boys. Most of them had celebrated their Bar Mitzvah or were about to do so. Bat Mitzvah for girls was not common in those days. The boys, in fairly advanced stage of puberty, were busy demonstrating their machismo through raucous behaviour and manifestation of indiscipline in class and outside the class A few of the more traditional teachers found the work with our group literally traumatic. They walked into the class fearing that some unexpected catastrophe would create havoc with their teaching programme.

One day the head of the school announced that a new biology teacher, by the name of Ephraim Katchalsky (EK for short) was joining the school. The class 'mafia' decided to plan some creative upheaval as a welcome to the new teacher and make him aware of the kind of undisciplined 'mob' we were. We felt that a new teacher ought to be 'trained' to recognise and accept our ideas of a relationship between teachers and pupils. He had to understand that we, the pupils, were in the driving seat. Much

Ephraim Katzir.

to our surprise EK had different ideas. He was young, energetic and had robust ideas about discipline. Unbeknown to us he undertook a thorough 'market research' to identify the main troublemakers in the class. The other teachers gave him a list of the main source of collective indiscipline and described what the guys looked like and where they sat in the class. The main alleged culprit was a boy called Rafi Sitton, whose pew was at the back and was always in the habit of leaning against the wall. Unmissable Rafi. He was the tallest in the class with a constant impertinent smirk. Without ceremony EK walked towards Rafi and told him to leave the room immediately. 'But I have not done anything wrong' remonstrated Rafi. 'Not yet, and moreover I won't give you a chance to do anything wrong.' From that point onwards the discipline in Katschalsky's lessons was exemplary. We learnt a lot and enjoyed EK's lessons. By the way Sitton was allowed eventually back. He ceased leaning against the wall and became a diligent student.

Ephraim Katschalsky changed his surname to Katzir. He became an eminent scientist and in 1973 became the President of Israel. He welcomed president Sadat to Israel to sign a peace treaty between Israel and Egypt. I felt privileged to be taught by him and due to his charismatic teaching I loved biology.

Can tyrants teach?

Yona in Hebrew is pigeon. Our teacher Yona was no pigeon by any stretch of the imagination. Mr. Yona was responsible for teaching us Hebrew literature, both ancient and modern. The ancient encompassed all poems, orations by biblical personalities like King David, prophets and well-known psalms. The modern included a plethora of poems, plays (or parts thereof) by living famous Hebrew poets like Bialik and Tchernichovsky.

As a class we were eager to learn but Mr. Yona was an impatient, intimidating tyrant with the result that the only pedagogical method at his disposal was fear. He never paid a compliment for good performance and enjoyed humiliating the student whose performance was not perfect.

The other educational strategy was making us 'memorise long passages from the bible or modern literature by heart'… Thus, for instance, he would announce: 'By next Sunday I want you all to memorise Bialik's famous poem 'Take me under your Wing' I shall invite a few of you, and at random, to recite it fully without hesitation, without interruptions, without mistakes and in a way which demonstrates your understanding of the mood of the poet when he wrote it.'

This was nightmare scenario. Learning a poem by heart is one thing but the list of pitfalls to avoid in front of a whole class verged on harassment. In today's social and educational environments our teacher could have faced serious admonition from above or even legal consequences.

Following the recitation of the piece in question by any boy or girl in our class came the miserable post-mortem tirade of disapproval. Mr. Yona could spend ages with a flowing diatribe that devastated the victims. He went on and on, and on occasions the victims even burst into tears. It all verged on verbal abuse. Mr. Yona was keen on the phrase 'Selecting candidates randomly…' This was a lie. In front of him he had the class register that listed us all alphabetically. He followed the alphabet step by step with religious ardour. .

This added to the angst of the whole class. Each one of us could pinpoint the arrival of the torture day. When all the 'B's' were tortured the turn of the 'C's' was quick to follow. I could time with precision the day when the 'M's' turn was round the corner. I decided to fight this abomination with passive resistance and a well-planned escape route from this potential excruciating torment. I was not going to let Mr. Yona humiliate me in front of the whole class.

My creative strategy was to be absent when my turn was about to take place in accordance with the non-random alphabetical list. Clearly, if I avoid being in the class on the day, I do not have to learn the poem or speech by-heart. What a relaxing thought!

Question: how do I play AOL? I shall be ill…

On the day of my potential torment and shame I announced at breakfast that I felt very unwell. Mother touched my forehead and, after slight hesitation, decided that a thermometer must be summoned. A thermometer was stuck into my mouth. Mother turned round to continue to prepare the breakfast and whilst she had her back to me I inserted the thermometer's mercury end into the recently boiled tea pot. Alas on quick inspection I was horrified to see that the reading jumped to 48 degrees. The patient is probably at death door.

I surreptitiously shook the thermometer to lower the reading and eventually settled for 39 degrees. It is above normal but not life-threatening. I satisfied my mother and a 'sickie note' signed by my doctor father was issued. This was a very successful escape. I realised of course that I cannot use this trick on a regular basis. My mother could not be hoodwinked with an elevated fever at breakfast time more than once. Nonetheless I was determined to engineer another escape ploy. I felt that the solution lay in manipulating the alphabetical register of the class students.

It so happened that every term one individual was given the task of looking after the register.

The main task was to keep the register up-to-date. If a pupil moved away his or her name had to be removed. New arrivals had to be added. With the prevalent fashion in the country of changing surnames to sound closer to Hebrew style the new names had to replace the old ones on the list.

Eureka! This might be the key to changing my identity from time to time. The register 'controller' was my good friend Motta. I used to help him to do his maths homework so he owed me one. I timed my move when Mr. Yona was approaching the Ms for the umpteenth time.

'Motta, my family have decided to change our surname from Majaro to Ben Ari – namely the 'Son of Lion'. Father being Leon and I am the Son of Leon (or Lion) it makes sense for me to be Ben Ari (Arie in Hebrew is Lion). Great! I would land in the 'B's' and escape the torment for a while. Later on I can juggle with the options and when suitable return to the 'M's'. Mr Yona will never notice how Majaro morphed into Ben Ari and vice versa.

Motta loved this trick and co-operated fully although it involved him in a lot of work in re-copying the rota list in its metamorphosed form. Suddenly the boring job of being the register keeper gained interesting and amusing nuances. On my part I defied successfully Mr. Yona's absurd system of learning pages upon pages by heart. Due to my devious dodge I had time to listen to music and read books. Thanks to cheeky scheming I extricated myself totally from Mr. Yona's nasty clutches.

Motta was a popular captain of our netball team. Later on, and after University, he joined the regular Army and ended as a successful IDF Chief of Staff. Alas he passed away fairly young as a result of an untreatable brain tumour.

SM: sex guru

The word SEX did not cross the lips of well-behaved people in our social milieu.

It was rare for parents to enlighten their children, at any stage, about the biological miracle of procreation. Young people were left to discover sexual realities by slow experimentation over a long period or gossiping with a network of school friends, who for some reason were better informed.

For a serendipitous reason I happened to become 'better informed', or at least I thought I was. It all confirmed the old adage that 'in the land of the blind a one-eyed man is king'. Inadvertently, and under false pretences, I became the sex guru of my school year.

By way of background I need to explain that at the age of 15 I became a very diligent and ambitious scholar.

While I strove to get to the top of the class I only succeeded to reach the second spot. At the top, and year after year, was a brilliant boy by the name of Yehuda Freiman. Reluctantly I had to admit to myself that he was brilliant all round. He had a most promising career ahead of him in every subject – both in the arts and science. He happened to be a close personal friend and I admired him greatly.

On finishing school, Yehuda volunteered to join the Palmach, the commando brigade of the Haganah and participated in many arduous and dangerous campaigns in the war of independence.

Tragically in a battle in an Arab village outside Jerusalem, he pulled the plug of a grenade and it exploded in his hand and he was mortally injured. I still mourn him with a heavy heart.

My personal ambition was to get good results in the Palestine Baccalaureate exams and also pass the London Matriculation, which could be taken externally on two occasions every year. Gaining a London Matriculation was the best route to a British university, which I aspired to join.

One of the subjects I chose for both exams was French. My spoken French was relatively fluent but I had problems with French grammar especially with the subjunctive tense.

I decided that the time has come to read as many French books as possible to gain fluency and enlarge my vocabulary. My father in his surgery attached to our apartment had shelves upon shelves of books, mostly in French. Many of these books were of medical technical nature and were of doubtful value to me and my French.

One book triggered my imagination: *Le Mariage*. This was an old-fashioned French book for young couples about to be married. Obviously my parents learnt all about love-making from this book.

It described in great detail and in clear language and drawings all about the sex act, the genitalia of both sexes, potential problems and other important matters to be followed towards a happy and fruitful marriage. I lapped it all up and looked forward to the opportunity of enlightening my school network (of course, boys only).

The one problem I encountered was that I bumped into words in French and I did not know their equivalent in Hebrew. After all my network audience were all Hebrew speakers. For instance, I did not know the Hebrew word for 'orgasm' ('orgasme in French). Moreover I could not ask anyone in the family. It was all a clandestine mission. On a few occasions I improvised new words and to that extent I enriched the Hebrew language vocabulary pertaining to sexual nomenclature. Me and Bialik. I decided to name orgasm in Hebrew as orgasmus. Who could challenge me at the time?

Duly equipped with what I believed was a semi-reliable story, coupled with pretty illustrations I decided to 'market' it to the male peers in my class. Instinct told me that I should have a very enthusiastic audience. I appointed two of my close pals to act as recruiting ambassadors. Strict conditions were attached to the membership of this secret mini club. The request to join this secret fraternity of pubescent club was overwhelming.

We arranged to meet in a furtive way, in a popular corner of the school's gym. In sessions of about 20 minutes we compared notes and imparted bits of extra 'knowledge' about the 'subject'.

We became a close-knit, rather elitist cabal of adolescents. Occasionally an odd teacher would notice us in our undercover meetings and wondered what nefarious conspiracy we were cooking. When asked we explained that we were following with interest the progress of the war in Europe (the Normandy invasion had taken place...)

The girls were mystified by this strange conclave but conceded that boys are boys and did not try to intrude.

Thus a group of 15- and 16-year-olds gained some insights into the virtual joys of sex via my enthusiasm to improve my French by ploughing through an old-fashioned book of marital bliss intended for newly-betrothed couples towards the end of the 19th Century.

My French improved although an antique sex book did not unravel for me the subtleties of the subjunctive tense. Nonetheless I passed all my exams and gained my two matriculations with distinction.

The truly amusing finale occurred about a decade later, when I already lived in London, and I informed my parents that I had become engaged to be married to dear Pamela. A neatly-packed parcel arrived from Jerusalem containing a book called Le Mariage – the same book which I almost knew by heart. It had my finger-prints on every page including the illustrations I copied so laboriously. I am a very proud owner of this relic of the past that no doubt helped my parents to conceive me.

Eli Auster

Eli (Eliyahu) Auster was the son of Daniel Auster, the first Jewish mayor of Jerusalem. Traditionally, and going back to the Ottoman period, the mayor of the city was always an Arab and a deputy was Jewish. With gradual change in the city's demography the British mandatory authorities decided, in consultation with the Jewish leadership, that it was appropriate to have a Jewish mayor. Auster got the job. He was the mayor when Israel gained its independence and was a signatory to the Declaration of Independence.

Auster was a skilful diplomat and managed to steer a comfortable relationship with his Arab colleagues in the municipality – not a mean achievement.

Auster's son Eli was a very close friend of mine from a very early age. We started our friendship at the kindergarten and moved simultaneously through the normal route of primary school, middle school and senior school. We studied together in the same schools and in the same classes for 14 years. I was a frequent visitor in their most elegant and luxurious apartment.

Eli's father Daniel Auster, the first Jewish Mayor of Jerusalem.

Eli's bedroom was littered with an amazing plethora of expensive toys and games. Coming to his den was like an exciting visit to a luxury and well-stocked toy shop. For me, and our other joint friends, it was always an exciting occasion to spend time in the Austers' flat. We could play with toys that none of us could dream of possessing in our respective homes.

As we were getting older Eli's possessions matured into more semi-adult items. The Auster's apartment was spacious and we were completely isolated from the rest of the family and staff. We were ensconced in a happy and secluded corner and left to ourselves.

In 1945, at the age of 16, on one of our traditional visits Eli asked the three of us to swear to secrecy. He was about to share with us a secret. We followed his request.

What was the secret? He pulled a small Beretta pistol out of a drawer.

We had no idea how he acquired this pistol. Did it belong to his father? Did he steal it from the armoury of the camp where we had to attend some compulsory pre-military exercises? Mystery!

Nonetheless it was great fun to play with a real pistol. I admired the precision work that went into making such a device. The various pieces that make a pistol fit so smoothly together. Slowly we got to know all the parts intimately but short of firing real bullets we got to know the revolver in detail. We were very careful in removing all the bullets while we were handling it. The risk of an accident was completely removed while we were studying it. We were playing safely with an adult toy.

Little we guessed at the time that we were fooling around with the source of an unimaginable tragedy.

A phone call from one of our inner cabal of friends broke the dreadful news. Eli shot himself and died.

Our world fell apart. Endless police investigations followed. Three of us were cross-examined for hours. We were all shattered.

The school organised a wake by the coffin. For 24 hours four of Eli's friends (including me) plus other students from our class took shifts of four hours each to stand by the coffin. When I was on duty Eli's mother Julia arrived in semi-demented state and screamed: 'Eli why did you do it? Why, Why?...

The tragedy landed in the hands of a coroner who, following police and medical reports concluded that it was an unfortunate accident. They averred that Eli was playing with the pistol and accidentally pressed the trigger.

We, his close friends, disagreed with this judgement. Eli knew the pistol inside out; he was always meticulous with the safety catch and the likelihood that he pressed the trigger accidentally was not plausible. We suspected that he had a big row with his parents and decided to use the pistol in order to cause a minor injury to himself and that gesture went terribly wrong.

I knew that Eli was invited to go on a kibbutz with the view of being trained as a junior Palmach cadet. (The Palmach was the Haganah's military wing) and his parents were adamant against it. They had many stormy arguments.

In our mind the mystery was never solved. The reality was that we lost a dear, dear friend.

'You work, you earn'

In our household the idea of giving the children pocket money was anathema.

Money had to be earned. From a very young age I was aware of the family's work ethics: in order to earn some cash I needed to perform a task ordained by one of my parents. Cleaning windows had one fee rate; tidying the garden had another rate. We were talking about very modest amounts but the principle was clear: 'You work, you earn'.

The result was that I learnt to respect the value of money. Having worked hard to earn it the urge to save, at least most of it, was strong. At the age of 10 I opened a Post Office savings account and enjoyed seeing the entries mounting every month by dribs and drabs. And WOW, twice a year the account added a bonus called interest.

The other result was that I was constantly in search of ideas of the kind of services I might offer to my parents or the network of acquaintances and colleagues in exchange for a suitable monetary award.

I conceived a plethora of diverse offerings. To my father I offered the service of editing his letters, reports and potential books, which he wrote in Hebrew. Father's spoken Hebrew was remarkably good but his written material needed careful editing for grammatical and syntactic errors. I became father's official Hebrew editor and was rewarded accordingly. It became a regular modest source of income.

At school I promoted the idea that I was prepared to give private tutoring, especially in maths, to pupils who needed a leg-up in coping with the subject. In this instance three candidates responded and I was commissioned and paid by their respective parents. I was highly gratified when all three passed their exams with satisfactory marks.

Of the three 'pupils' one became a top general in the Israel Defence Force (IDF); one became a judge and the third, who was an excellent musician, became a life-long member of the Israel Philharmonic Orchestra. I met the latter two many years later. Sadly the general shot himself when told that he had an incurable brain tumour resulting in unbearable continuous headaches.

My reputation as a competent tutor was greatly enhanced and extra work followed. my portfolio of external work started interfering with my own school homework. Reluctantly I had to ration the available time for the 'you work, you earn' activities.

Following my two apprenticeship periods with the local cabinet maker I was often invited by friends of my parents to undertake DIY jobs. These jobs ranged from simple plumbing to some repairs to furniture. I became the Jerusalem 'fixer' and earned fairly lavish pocket money.

While I was very thrifty with my 'you work; you earn' income I could afford to fulfil a long-wished dream to learn the basics of mechanical drawings. I bought a beautiful set of drawing instruments, but I needed some guidance how to draw a cylinder; how to draw a sphere; how to draw a cube and altogether muster drawing techniques.

My research located a part-time evening course for beginners. It was spread over six weeks and lasted about four hours every Tuesday evening. I booked for it with my parents' encouragement and loved every minute of it.

Complex items, like engine components, were placed on a table in front of the class and we had the task of measuring every dimension carefully and draw it on paper.

During the course the items we needed to draw became more and more complex, including spiral shapes, and drawing them accurately was a real challenge.

I took to the whole process like a fish to water and achieved fairly high standard of draftsmanship.

After the course I mounted dozens of these drawings into a large album and I am still proud to see the quality I achieved. This album is still in my possession and so is the set of drawing instruments I invested in prior to the course.

I became a proficient mechanical draftsman. I received a diploma to testify that I attended and passed all the needed requirements with great honour.

One occasion for which the 'you work; you earn' policy became most apt happened when I was around 15 years old. It related to music.

My parents were very anxious for me to learn to play an instrument. From the age of 8 I was given piano lessons with a Hungarian lady by the name of Mrs. Rubitchek. I hated her, I hated her lessons and I was making very little progress. I used to hide under the bed when I heard her coming and my mother had to drag me from my hiding place to attend the lesson. After three years of reluctant learning I could manage to play a poor rendition of Beethoven's Fur Elise and an even poorer version of the Blue Danube Waltz. It was evident that I was not a music wunderkind in the making.

My mother reached a very rational but sad decision: 'You do not enjoy the lessons; you do not practise between lessons; you make pitiful progress... Let us call it a day and stop the lessons. However if you ever fancy learning to play an instrument you will have to pay for the lessons yourself out of your own cash flow.' This became a clear agreement between us and I adhered to it ever since.

I was very happy to stop the piano lessons with Mrs. Rubitchek but at the same time I felt that I let my mother down. She was so keen to develop in me and my sister a high level of musicianship and I frustrated that ambition of hers.

A few years later I developed the wish to play the violin. That was a watershed in my love for music. I remembered the deal I struck with my mother about me paying for the lessons. Father very kindly allowed me to play on his beloved Stradivarius Fecit violin. I consulted a few of my friends who had violin lessons and visited a few potential teachers. I met them all and selected a teacher with whom I struck a pleasant rapport. I negotiated a fee rate and started my violin lessons with enthusiasm and diligence. I paid for the lessons from that point onwards.

On reflection I concluded that it was an excellent formula for choosing a teacher. Let the young pupil research and find his or her own teacher.

I had wonderful lessons with Dov Avital. I stayed with him for a few years until the war broke out and I needed to move from Jerusalem.

I made giant progress, took grade exams in the local conservatoire and loved every minute of it. I pondered: 'What did Mrs. Rubishek do wrong to antagonise me so thoroughly.' Maybe I was too young when I started with her.

My violin teacher taught me the first rudiments of chamber music and very often we played duets together for two violins.

Dov Avital created a miracle for me – I learnt to enjoy playing scales! He encouraged me to go the chamber music concerts at the glorious YMCA amphitheatre.

The idea that I was paying for all the lessons out of my own savings boosted my self-esteem considerably. I was in the driving seat in relation to my own music education.

Instruments made by Simon Majaro:
Violin after Stradivarius, 1716. Viola after Magginni.

Apprenticed to Pinky the cabinet-maker

At the end of our road a cabinet-maker Pinky (short for Pinhas) ran a workshop for designing and making high quality 'made-to-measure' furniture.

For years we were on nodding acquaintance relationship. Every time I came back from school I passed by his workshop and we greeted each other warmly. Yet we never entered into any dialogue or conversation. Nonetheless I admired the quality of his work, which I could detect through his wide-open front double-door. I was envious of his talent and skill and the joy of producing such beautiful handiwork. A few of our neighbours had their entire internal furnishing designed and made by him and his small number of assistants.

Short time after my 14th birthday, and at the beginning of the school summer holidays, my father came home with an amazing surprise: 'Pinky, the carpenter down the road, stopped me on my way home and asked if Simon would be interested in working for him during the summer school holidays for £1 a week'... £1 a week in 1943 was a lot of money for a young boy. This was an offer I could not refuse. Besides, working for the great Pinky, the cabinet-maker, what a joy!

I knew little as to how this offer came about and how my father's contact with Pinky happened. I was too excited to probe for a full background to the offer. The main, very exciting fact was that I was offered a 'job' for £1 a week to assist the wonderful cabinet-maker that I admired so much.

This two-month relationship happened twice, in two running summers. It was a true 'apprenticeship' that helped to form my character and equipped me with skills and work ethos that affected all my future adult life.

As a preamble to the whole episode I did not know at the time that my father had engineered it all. He was worried that I might waste precious time during the summer break and spend too much time with friends on useless activities. He was the one who approached Pinky with the offer: 'Give Simon a job for which I would ask you to pay him £1 a week and I shall pay you £2 a week.' A win-win deal all round.

I only discovered this cunning arrangement many years later.

My father's motivation in this regard was based on a sad reality that befell his own father following the Bolshevik take-over. My father's father, Simion Mojarowsky, was a lawyer and director and part-owner of the best-known newspaper in Odessa, Odesky Novosti. He led a comfortable life with great social prestige.

With the arrival of communism his newspaper was nationalised and he lost his job and income. In a matter of weeks he was reduced to penury. Moreover Odessa was in the throes of a nasty famine and every item of food cost a fortune.

The fascinating story goes on to recount how my grandfather Simion taught himself to make ladies' shoes of some quality and elegance.

He started from zero knowledge and had to improvise simple tools. Yet he managed, slowly, to make ladies shoes and gained the reputation in the circumstances of being a good maker. Selling these shoes or bartering for needed supplies provided him with a modest income to sustain himself and his wife.

The moral of the story convinced my father that every person should acquire, at an early age, a physical craft and skill to use in emergencies such as political and social upheavals. The whole project equipped me with a woodworking skill, which served me well for the rest of my life, both for DIY purposes and for stimulating hobby projects such as violin making.

For his part Pinky took the whole project very seriously. Rather than allowing me to mess about in the workshop and make the occasional coffee, he decided to mentor and train me as a true apprentice. He planned it carefully with patience and open heart.

As a first step he produced for me a written woodworkers' list of commandments:

1. *All the tools must be sharp at all times.* He taught me how to sharpen tools with the various devices available. I did not know of the amazing array of stones that are available to a wood

worker, varying from a diamond studded stone to a so-called Arkansas stone. Choosing the most appropriate stone is a skill in itself.

I learnt how to sharpen tools to high standard of sharpness and, much to my surprise, I developed a passion for the whole process. Holding a very sharp scraper in one's hand is quite exciting. I spent many hours sharpening tools of the workshop and loved doing it.

2. *Always enjoy what you are doing. If you do not enjoy performing a task the output is unlikely to be the best.* I found it difficult to cope with this edict. I felt that boring is boring – how can you enjoy a boring job? Yet I gradually discovered that every boring challenge has a silver lining. By improvising a fresh routine a nasty job can open new opportunities towards excellence. It all needs a modicum of optimism.

3. *Don't be afraid of improvising to solve problems.* You are bound to encounter challenges during carpentry work. In search of solutions do not flinch from improvising .This advice helped me enormously on many occasions and improved my creative thinking.

4. *Measure, measure, measure frequently.* This was a wonderful piece of advice. An error in measurement ignored at an early stage can often lead to a 'time bomb' problem later on. This became patently obvious to me years later when I started making violins. Lutherie is an unforgiving activity. A small error in measurement can lead to endless complications at a later date.

5. *Improve your patience.* 'Woodworking needs unlimited patience' was Pinky's top commandment. While I possess a modicum of patience it is far from unlimited. Yet I admired Pinky and respected his philosophies.

Whenever circumstances tested my patience I recalled Pinky's wise word and muttered to myself: 'calm down and remember Pinky's commandment'. Gradually it became part of my personal ethos towards work and my patience burgeoned. This improvement remained with me ever since.

Pinky was a delightful mentor. He accepted his role to train me with enthusiasm and friendship. My two summer periods in his atelier had an enormous impact on me as a teenager and served me well for the rest of my life. I became a fairly competent woodworker.

During my so-called apprenticeship period I produced a couple of handsome three-legged chairs and an ice box.

This latter project was my pièce de résistance of which the whole family were proud. At the time having a refrigerator was a rare luxury. I decided to make an ice box that looked like a refrigerator but needed to be filled with blocks of ice, which a local ice vendor supplied in our area every Friday.

I designed an ice box with suitable inner insulation. I studied the very large and complex insulation industry and settled for cellulose boards, which were easily available and had outstanding insulation properties. I also had to locate hinges and snap-on handle. It looked great and the family loved it. The acid test of quality was the fact that a small block of ice bought on Friday lasted the whole week! It served my family for a few years until progress made them purchase an electric refrigerator. My ice box remained as a museum piece in the centre of my parents' apartment but lost its role as the family's cooling device and food preserver.

When ignorance is bliss, 'tis folly to be wise

A short while after the disappearance and death of my dear cat Mitzi my mother decided that we ought to get one or two chickens with the intention of having our own source of fresh eggs. The idea was to get a flow of fresh eggs and also distract me from moping over the loss of my pet.

In reality no member of our family knew anything about the egg-laying biology of chickens. Our ignorance on the subject was total. We argued endlessly on whether hens would lay eggs without a rooster around. I took the view, wrongly, that the presence of a cockerel is essential.

As I was the only woodworker in the family I was given the task of erecting a chicken coop in the garden to house a new arrival. I thoroughly enjoyed this part of the project. In a matter of days I erected a very welcoming home for the hens.

Mother and I went to the famous Makhne Yehuda market to purchase a hen or two. Mustafa, the Arab vendor, 'saw us coming', as they say, and detected immediately our ignorance and innocence. He offered us a pretty little chicken with an

The loss of a pet and a desire for eggs inspired us to buy a chicken.

assurance that she laid eggs every day. He showed us, in a nearby basket a few healthy looking eggs and swore on Allah that they were hers. After an inevitable short haggling session we reached a compromise price, shook hands and marched back home with a chicken.

In order to create an immediate friendly rapport with the new member of the family we decided to call her Nora.

Nora seemed reasonably happy in her new home. I fed her with an assortment of grains and other healthy foods. I left a small dish with water. I got straw to make the coop ground more comfortable. Nora had everything she needed to meet her physical needs. All that was required from her was eggs.

Every morning I rushed to the coop to see whether an egg was laid. Alas no eggs. This went on for days and weeks. No eggs. Mistakenly I assumed the role of an expert. I persisted with my theory that a hen needs a cockerel to produce eggs. My parents insisted that I was wrong.

Eventually my mother and I trooped again to the Makhne Yehuda market to see if Mustafa was still there. Indeed he was there and purported to be pleased to see us.

We expressed our disappointment that lovely Nora failed to present us with eggs. 'Ah, said Mustafa, you need a cock'... so I was right. Another set of negotiations and we returned home with a very handsome cockerel. So now we had a couple – male and female. The cockerel needed a name and we called him Oli (for Oliver).

Nora and Oli were a strange couple. They ignored each other and stuck to separate corners of the coop. When I spread a small pile of grain Nora would not let Oli come near it.

Meanwhile we still did not get any eggs,

I started worrying about their respective sexuality.

The whole project became highly suspect.

Both my parents were talking about cutting our loses and withdrawing from the whole venture. Having invested so much time and money in the whole project I resisted the idea of aborting it prematurely. We had a coop, a chicken, a cockerel – surely eggs would follow...

I decided to stop my parents from being so dispirited about the prospects. They needed some fillip to re-kindle their enthusiasm for our egg-laying future.

I went to the market on my own and bought an egg. I made a mistake by choosing one of the cheaper ones.

I came home with an egg and furtively deposited it in the coop. Oli ignored the fact that an egg was lying on the floor of the coop. On the other hand Nora marched around it and every now and again pecked at it with her sharp beak. She looked obfuscated as if she had doubts about the authenticity of the egg. If she could speak she would announce 'This egg is not mine'. Obviously chickens are more intelligent than we think.

I decided not to announce the existence of an egg in the coop to my mother. The next morning whilst I was away at school my mother went to the garden to inspect the coop and apparently jumped with joy 'Hooray' we have an egg! This refrain greeted me on my return from school. I was offered to be the first to eat and enjoy Nora's freshly laid egg. I bit my tongue and kept *shtum*, wondering how long I could keep this charade going.

Next morning, for breakfast, the egg was ceremoniously boiled for four minutes and I was the lucky person to savour it. On breaking the shell a slightly rancid odour wafted into my nose. My alter ego chastised me for having bought the cheapest egg in the first place.

As a punishment for having manipulated such a devious trick I ate quickly the egg in spite of its obvious doubtful freshness. I thought if I die I deserve it. That was the first and last egg in the coop.

Unexpectedly a major problem arose. Oli had a most powerful crowing voice. Moreover he rehearsed it every morning between 3.00 and 4.00.

Unfortunately my coop was right next door to our neighbour's bedroom.

Our neighbour, Amnon Orbach, was a reserve Major in the IDF. He got angrier and angrier and even threatened to shoot Oli with the Uzi sub-machine gun, which he had at home. He also threatened to get lawyers to complain to the Town Hall and make our life a misery.

This was the last straw. My parents decided to act quickly and terminate our egg-laying enterprise.

Back to Mustafa they sold Oli and received half of what they had paid. No doubt Mustafa would sell it again at full price to similar mugs.

Nora was slaughtered and served for dinner on a Friday night. I refused to partake. I considered it as cannibalism. The rest of the family enjoyed it thoroughly.

My chicken farming experience ended in total disgrace. My knowledge of hen-breeding biology is still in a semi-ignorant mode.

The bombing of the King David Hotel in Jerusalem brought an end to a friendship.

British Library and a pen friend in London

Throughout my school days I was determined to perfect my English. My aim was to sit the London Matriculation exams, which were held in Jerusalem twice a year. The London Matriculation on top of the Palestine equivalent more or less guaranteed admittance to an English University.

At school I had a lovely English lady teacher by the name of Mrs. Tepper. I revered her. She originated from the UK and she and her family immigrated to Jerusalem. She was aware of my enthusiasm to improve my English and I became her pet student. She felt that what I needed was an English speaker with whom I could converse in English. My written English was good but I needed some practice to improve my spoken language. One day Mrs. Tepper presented to me two very interesting ideas. First she explained that the British Council had opened a library in Jerusalem and one of the librarians, Mandy McManus, a young English girl she knew well, was prepared to meet me and hold conversations in English. Mandy did not speak Hebrew so it guaranteed that we had to chat in English.

The second idea, she explained that she was asked by a friend in London whether any of her students would be prepared to act as a 'pen friend' with a Jewish English student. I said I would love to. Very soon after that conversation I was given the name and address of a London Jewish girl by the name of Renee W, who became a dear Pen Friend for five years until I met her in person when I finally landed in London.

Mrs. Tepper made arrangements for these initiatives and I took to both like a fish to water.

With some hesitation I took the long walk from school to the British Council Library. I warned my mother that I might be late because on Mrs. Tepper's advice I went to British Council Library to pick up a few English books.

On arrival I saw two librarians – one looked like my mother's age and one looked very young and most attractive. I decided that the young one was Mandy. I introduced myself whilst trying to suppress my timidity. Mandy, who was probably two years older than me, was very confident and knew who I was and put me at ease instantly. This was the beginning of a most exciting platonic love.

Mandy was the daughter of a senior department head in the government's civil service. The British expatriates in Palestine had their own schools and social network. As a result their children had very little contact with the 'natives' and their kids. Fraternising with me was a novel experience for both Mandy and me. Our relationship developed into an extraordinary pure literary rapport.

Mandy insisted on calling me Simon rather Shimon. She prepared a whole menu of books that I ought to borrow and read and subsequently discuss with her. We started with Thomas Hardy's classics. I read avidly Tess of the d'Urbervilles, Far from the Madding Crowd and The Mayor of Casterbridge. Every time I brought a book back I underwent Mandy's gentle and instructive cross-examination of my reaction to each book, its style, characters and the author's genre of writing. Mandy behaved almost as a professional teacher throughout with incredible patience and charm. I was constantly longing to hug her.

This amazing literary relationship lasted around eighteen months. It was spotlessly platonic. The only marginal symbol of our intimacy on my part was a gentle pet on one of her cheeks, which caused us both to blush.

During that period I started my correspondence with RW, my pen-friend in London. We got into a routine of sending on average two letters a month. Mandy agreed to act as an editor of my letters and remove errors and altogether polish my style. The result was that my letters were perfect, much to the surprise of my friend in London. She was amazed that a boy in Jerusalem could write such fine letters in English. Bravo Mandy! When RW and I eventually met in London I never admitted to her that behind my perfect letters I had my private 'Cyrano de Bergerac' acting as an eloquent proof-reader.

Whilst I was enjoying this wonderful friendship with Mandy the world around us was in state of turmoil. A murderous

Jewish terrorist insurgency against the British Mandatory Government and institutions was masterminded by two ruthless militias: the Irgun and the so-called Stern Gang. Various military and governmental establishments were bombed. On their part the army and police retaliated with a campaign of harassment of the Jewish communities. Random arrests and house-to-house searches for terrorists or their sympathisers made life in Jerusalem fraught and young men were careful not to be seen in the centre of the town late at night.

On Monday, 22 July 1946 the most brutal attack on the British Government's headquarters was perpetrated by the Irgun. The southern wing of the famous King David Hotel in Jerusalem, which housed the government's headquarters in the country was blown up with a heavy toll of dead among the civil service and military personnel. This was the deadliest terrorist outrage directed at the British during the Mandate era (1920–1948). The relationship between the British authorities and the Jewish establishment became very tense and never recovered until the British left Palestine in 1948. Although the outrage was carried out by a splinter group of terrorists the Government inflicted a series of punishments on the whole Jewish community.

Indirectly I happened to be a victim of this dreadful event. Mandy's family were ordered to leave Jerusalem and return to Britain. I lost my lovely friend and English mentor. I was bereft and sadly never heard anything from her. Our romance got blown up with the King David Hotel.

The slow road to hell

Events in the Holy Land were moving at an alarming pace. The British Government was totally exasperated by the political gridlock and the upsurge of militancy on all sides. They decided to opt out of the Palestinian quagmire and hand over the whole issue to the United Nations for some adjudication regarding the future of the country.

The whole situation evoked among the Jewish community a myriad of views and opinions as to the strategic direction that its leadership ought to pursue in the light of a vacuum about to happen on the departure of the British army and administration.

Opinions varied enormously. At one extreme support was aired, especially by Irgun supporters, for the brutal concept of ethnic cleansing of the Arab villages and towns that neighboured Jewish communities and posed a serious danger. At the other extreme were adherents to the notion that a true dialogue could be achieved provided the right Arab interlocutors could be identified.

I was at the time in my last year of the senior school and about to take the Baccalaureate exams.

The debate about the future pervaded our lives.

Like the population outside the school our views covered the full range of potential strategies from 'let's kill them all' to 'let's make big efforts to talk'.

The school did not have an official stated view on the subject. A few of the teachers, especially the younger ones, who happened to be clandestine part-time Haganah officers, were quite happy to articulate strong antipathy to the Arabs in general. Their deeply-felt mantra was the Zionist dream: 'This country is ours – to hell with those who try to put obstacles to our dream…'

This atmosphere caused me a lot of anguish and heart-searching. I was brought up in a family in which Arabs were respected and we were in social contact with many. My father as a GP in the Old City treated many Arabs and they all loved him. He loved their simplicity and loyalty. My father coined the phrase: 'An Arab patient never asks for a second opinion…' We understood the many grievances that soured the Arabs' attitude but we respected their work ethic and reliability when treated well.

My sister and I were encouraged to learn Arabic and for a number of years we had regular lessons every Friday with an eminent teacher by the name of Ribchi Kemal. Mr Kemal was an impressive gentleman who had mastered the Hebrew language to perfection. This was rare among Arabs at the time.

Ribchi and his family were victims of the exodus of Arab refugees during the War of Independence. They escaped to Syria where he got immediately a job on the national broadcasting system to spread hate and poison in Hebrew for the world Jews and Israel. The transition from a loyal friend to a hating opponent was understandable in the circumstances.

My confusion was exacerbated during the so-called UNSCOP (United Nations Committee on Palestine), which was set up following Britain's announcement of their intention to quit Palestine and delegated this 'hot potato' to the UN.

The UN held most of their meetings in the YMCA tower block in Jerusalem and they were open to the public. I attended many of these meetings and it became clear to me from the many speeches by Arab and Jewish leaders that the gulf between the two sides was unbridgeable.

Two speakers impressed me enormously by their clear forensic analysis of the situation and their potential visions. The first was an academic by the name of Prof. Yehuda Magnes. The second, Prof. Martin Buber. Magnes, originally from the USA, was one of the founders of the Hebrew University and became its chancellor and later its president. Martin Buber was an eminent philosophy professor and prolific author.

These two gentlemen and a few other notables launched a couple of pressure groups: 'Ihud' (unity in Hebrew) and 'Brit Shalom'. I joined both as the youngest member. I liked their stated missions. Both groups were dedicated to the idea that Palestine should be neither Jewish nor Arab. Rather, they

Left: Yehuda Magnes. *Right*: Martin Buber

advocated a binational state in which equal rights would be shared by all. Poor Magnes was heckled by the university students when he made a speech to open the university year.

Altogether he had to face constant attacks from politicians and normal citizens. I was very hurt on his behalf.

Geography and geopolitics were among my favourite subjects. I researched avidly for a country that found a harmonious existence despite of its multifarious social, linguistic, demographic and ethnic strata.

Switzerland appeared to be the perfect model.

Few people realise what a combative and bellicose country Switzerland was centuries ago. The various cantons were in constant military conflict and the hostilities broadened to include close neighbours like Italy and the Habsburg empire. For the Swiss, over that period, fighting became almost a vocation. Not surprisingly in later years the Swiss 'marketed' themselves as professional mercenaries including the Swiss regiments that traditionally protect the Pope.

Reading a lot about Swiss history I came to the conclusion that the various regions known as cantons were exhausted and fed up with all the wars and were seeking an acceptable ending to fighting. I was hoping that war-fatigue could ultimately bring the Jews and the Arabs to a meaningful negotiating forum.

Major events took place when the emperor of the Habsburgs died. A few Swiss regions took their chance and met to enter into a permanent alliance in order to become independent and peaceful: the cantons of Schwyz, Unterwalden and Uri formed the Swiss Confederation on 1 August 1291. This mini confederation was so successful that other cantons queued to join. Gradually the Switzerland we know today emerged as a prosperous, peaceful and neutral nation – a model to be replicated. Switzerland has 26 cantons all living happily together in a confederation.

I discussed it with Prof. Magnes and he loved it. I became his pet. His own approach to the Jewish authorities on the whole subject was a bit aggressive and uncompromising with the result that he was sidelined. They simply ignored him. Even Albert Einstein was against him. For my part I continued to develop slowly my Swiss model and the way it could work in Palestine.

The idea was to establish a confederation with central parliament in Jerusalem and give the vote to each resident, regardless of religion or faith. The vote based on one person one vote. Parliament would elect a central government responsible for finance, defence and foreign affairs.

The country would be divided into cantons responsible for total local administration and services. The division into cantons would be recommended by a group of independent wise personalities from the outside and based on the majority of either Jews or Arabs in every designated canton. Minorities in each canton would enjoy full rights and will be entitled to vote for their cantonal government. The Swiss model could be copied to include its constitution (subject to suitable amendments), system of governance, electoral system both for the federation and the cantons, and include their very effective referendum system.

I realised that many changes would need to take place first, especially in the leadership of both sides, before the idea could be accepted and fostered.

After the Declaration of Independence of Israel in 1948 Prof. Magnes returned to the USA a sick man and shortly afterwards passed away. I missed an inspiring friend and mentor. He treated me as an adult and as a friend.

One major event took place on 29 November 1947: the long-winded deliberations of the UN Committee decided to partition Palestine into two discrete entities: Arab and Jewish. Jerusalem to become an international city. It was not entirely clear exactly what that meant. Little was said about the governance style of the two entities. Students on an MBA course at my university could have done a much better job. The division of the country into Jewish and Arab zones was a hodge-podge of non-contiguous areas. It was impossible to imagine how a medley of non-neighbouring areas could be managed as a state. Imagine Northumberland and Surrey being part of a single state!

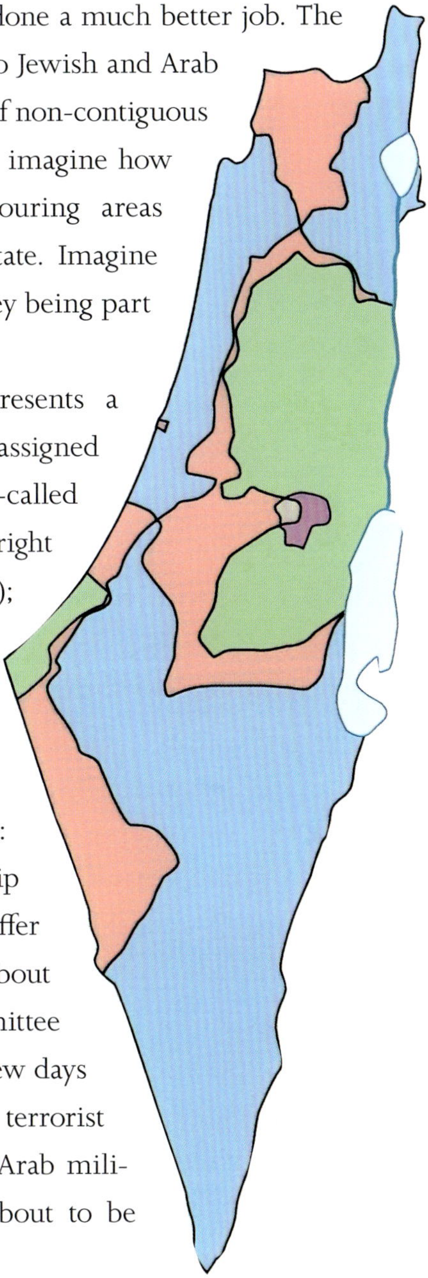

In this map blue represents a Jewish State; red and green assigned for an Arab state (The so-called West Bank green on the right to be controlled by Jordan); Jerusalem to become an international city. What that meant was left very unclear.

The inevitable followed: the Zionist leadership accepted the plan on offer subject to negotiation about details; the Arab committee rejected it outright and a few days later a series of murderous terrorist activities were started by Arab militias. The civil war was about to be unleashed.

The tension mounted and we all expected very sombre days ahead.

On 9 April 1948 a shameful, cataclysmic event took place which shattered my faith in what I always believed was the supremacy of Jewish moral code and human decency: the outrageous massacre in Deir Yassin.

The Deir Yassin atrocity will remain a permanent blot on Jewish conscience and psyche.

After sunset on 9 April 1948, 120 fighters from the two notorious militant paramilitary groups Irgun and Lehi (Stern Gang) descended on Deir Yassin, a village of about 600 inhabitants near Jerusalem, and massacred men, women and children in a most brutal way. Conflicting reports emerged on the number of casualties. The figures varied between 105 and 200 dead plus many injured.

The most gruesome side-show was when the assailants forced villagers into a truck and paraded them through the streets of West Jerusalem the next day.. The public's suspicion was that afterwards they were all butchered.

This catastrophic and shameful event was the trigger point for the mass exodus of thousands of Palestinian Arabs from many towns and villages thus creating the massive refugee problem that plagued all future attempts to negotiate some honourable solution to the Palestine logjam.

Surprisingly among the public at large the Deir Yassin massacre had some misguided supporters who felt that it provided the Arabs with a clear message that Jews can also behave in a barbaric way. This message fomented terror and panic among the Arabs in the vicinity of various areas that the partition plan had allocated to the Jews.

A few days later a group of Arab militants attacked an armoured bus carrying doctors, nurses and students on the way to the Hadassah Hospital in Mount Scopus and killed all the passengers – twenty in total. The Arabs claimed that it was in response to Deir Yassin. Tit-for-tat atrocities became a daily occurrence.

In the midst of these murky scenarios I still had two more school terms before finishing school and sitting for the graduation exams.

Our history and world affairs teacher DZ (I prefer not to give the true initials for a reason which will become clear later) gave us all a project: an essay on the subject 'Our country in 20 years'.

It is appropriate to mention that at this point we were only a few weeks before a declaration of independence was about to be proclaimed. The general fear was that after a declaration of independence all the Arab neighbours: Egypt, Syria, Jordan, Lebanon, Iraq, would move their forces into Palestine and a full war would be unleashed. In the middle of this we had to write an essay about 'our country in twenty years'.

Knowing our teacher DZ and his views I assumed that he wanted an avalanche of nationalistic and patriotic Zionist drivel. He was one of the apologists for the Deir Yassin massacre. I decided to express my own honest views and not 'play to the gallery'.

I started by stating that if we cannot reach honourable and mutually satisfactory accommodation with our Arab neighbours we are heading for a restless future plagued by constant wars – large and small.

I then decided to offer a detailed description of my pet solution in the form of a major amendment to the UN Partition plan under the title a 'Swiss Model'.

Briefly I asserted that the UN partition for two states, Jewish and Arab, based on the proposed land allocation to both parties was a non-starter for many reasons which I listed in detail.

In particular I opposed strongly the hopeless lack of contiguity among a few of the portions allocated to each side.

At that point I emphasised that if we decide to move to a Swiss Model the UN partition plan could be salvaged, at least in parts. The lack of contiguity among territories becomes less important.

We should abandon the ill-conceived idea of a two-state model. Under the Swiss model the country will become a confederation with its capital in Jerusalem. A parliament elected by all the citizens regardless of their religion or ethnic background will appoint a cabinet responsible for the governance of the country and especially responsible for finance, defence and foreign affairs.

The country will be divided into a series of semi-autonomous cantons. A modified UN partition plan could provide the basis of territorial allocation to each canton. At this level one can structure cantons with Arab majority and cantons with

Jewish majority. Each canton would manage its administration and services almost like an independent mini-state. The only constraints on this freedom would be the finance, defence and foreign portfolios, which would be managed by the central confederation.

Altogether the outcome should represent a happy combination of decentralisation at cantonal level and centralisation at the confederaion level for a small range, albeit important, functions.

I went to a lot of trouble to assemble a detailed road map for implementation. The gist of my essay was that if a decision is taken to adopt this route we ought to study carefully the Swiss constitution and its governance and jurisprudential styles of both the confederation and the cantons and try to emulate slowly all their successful features. 'Let us create the Switzerland of the middle east' was my very unorthodox message.

In political terms I believed that this approach might appeal to the more sober and sane leaderships of both sides.

I submitted my essay realising that Mr. DZ would not share my enthusiasm for my approach. My idea did not offer ethnic cleansing of whole Arab areas...

Ten days later the essays were returned with short comments of congratulation or critique for each of the essays. Those that offered implacable and iron-fisted anti-Arab scenarios got extra accolades. One by one the essays were returned to their authors. Mine was left to the bitter end.

'Now I have one paper left. I did not believe my eyes when I started reading it. The author abdicated from all the cherished Zionist dreams of having a Jewish state in the holy land. All he is prepared to offer are Jewish mini-statelets called cantons side-by-side with Arab cantons. Moreover the author belongs to a family that acted as pioneers promoting the active development of Jewish presence in the country. Grandfather was one of the founders of Tel Aviv; uncle was the mayor of Tel Aviv for 30 tears. Shame on you…'

…At this point he tossed my essay in the air towards me. It fell next to my desk. I was furious but decided to retain my dignity and calm. I got up, picked up my paper, and marched out of the classroom and slammed the door behind me. I walked out of school and never crossed the front door again.

I walked home and much to my surprise I felt liberated.

On reaching home I reported to my parents the full story and announced that I was not going back to the famous Hebrew Gymnasia.

My parents were wonderful. They gave me full support and encouragement. My father phoned the headteacher and told him that I was not coming back. The head made some enquiries and contacted us with a feeble excuse that there must have been some misunderstanding… 'No, sir, there was no misunderstanding. It was a case of heartless autocracy and closed mind. My son is not returning to such a narrow-minded environment in which Deir Yassin is good and peaceful Swiss model is bad.'

My picture, on walking out of school.

This was an unhappy end to my otherwise happy school days. I immediately devoted time to file applications for taking the Palestine Baccalaureate and the London University Matriculation exams externally. The Baccalaureate external exams took place on the same day as the ones taken by my erstwhile colleagues at school. The papers were the same. The only difference was that the external exams were held in a separate venue. I earned 'distinction' in all subjects in both exams.

My path towards the next academic stage opened in front of me. My walking out of school in a huff with my head high caused me no harm.